Thomas Hardy, Florence Henniker

In Scarlet and Grey

Stories of Soldiers and Others

Thomas Hardy, Florence Henniker

In Scarlet and Grey
Stories of Soldiers and Others

ISBN/EAN: 9783337133092

Printed in Europe, USA, Canada, Australia, Japan

Cover: Foto ©ninafisch / pixelio.de

More available books at **www.hansebooks.com**

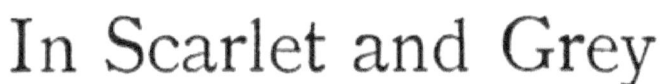

In Scarlet and Grey

STORIES OF SOLDIERS AND OTHERS BY

Florence Henniker

AND

THE SPECTRE OF THE REAL BY

Thomas Hardy and Florence Henniker

LONDON: JOHN LANE, VIGO ST
BOSTON: ROBERTS BROS., 1896

TO MY HUSBAND

THESE STORIES

ARE DEDICATED

CONTENTS

	PAGE
THE HEART OF THE COLOUR-SERGEANT,	1
BAD AND WORTHLESS,	30
A SUCCESSFUL INTRUSION,	52
A PAGE FROM A VICAR'S HISTORY,	103
AT THE SIGN OF THE STARTLED FAWN,	127
IN THE INFIRMARY,	150
THE SPECTRE OF THE REAL,	164

THE HEART OF
THE COLOUR SERGEANT

If two lives join, there is oft a scar,
They are one and one, with a shadowy third;
One near one is too far.

CHAPTER I

MISS KITTY MALONE had tied up the last bunch of carnations which smelt like ripe apricots newly gathered. She had arranged as a row of footlights beneath her, many flower-pots holding calceolarias and tufts of the little creeping plant familiarly known as 'Creeping Jenny.' Above Kitty's fair head a gigantic sunflower stood on a shelf, with attendant satellites in the shape of, golden and bronze dahlias and orange lilies. Miss Malone shook some of the pollen that had fallen from the last-named plants off the creamy lace at her wrists; and then, after pinning one small nosegay of forget-me-nots among the pale blue folds of her dress, she sat down, like a Queen of the May among her garlands, and waited for customers.

The large hall was very empty, although the church clock had rung out four half an hour ago. A sense of disappointment weighed down the spirits of some two dozen ladies, who, wearing business-like muslin aprons and scissors fastened at their waists, cast impatient eyes at the great doorway, and over a few aimless strollers who had passed through it.

'It's ten thousand pities,' said Miss O'Shaughnessy, who presided over pincushions and photograph frames under a canopy next to Miss Malone, 'that the Lord Lieutenant found at the last moment that he couldn't open the sale.' She spoke with a suspicion of a brogue, and pronounced her *ens* like *uns*. Then she looked sideways and not altogether agreeably at Kitty.

Miss O'Shaughnessy had been a reigning beauty in her beloved native city until the last season, when Miss Malone had come over to stay with a barrister uncle in Merrion Square, and had calmly taken away most of Miss O'Shaughnessy's favourite partners, and also her reputation as the prettiest girl at many balls and the cheerful race-meetings at Baldoyle and Fairyhouse. It could not be said that Kitty seemed elated overmuch after her triumphs: on the contrary, she received all admiration with a placid sense of its being no more than her due, and never exerted herself to win either attention or praise. Miss O'Shaughnessy's bitterness had reached its height a month or two ago at a small dance, when she had seen her rival led through a quadrille by the Lord Lieutenant, and taken in to supper by the Commander-in-Chief.

And just towards the close of that memorable evening, slangy Colonel Haldane, who had formerly been Miss O'Shaughnessy's most devoted admirer, had lounged across the room, and merely said, 'Heard the news?'

'No, what is it?'

'Well, the lovely Miss Malone has settled to make some fellow happy at last. She's accepted Vincent Pelham—thundering good marriage, ain't it? Capital soldier, old Vincent, though an awful dull dog. But his father ain't likely to hang on long, and then he'll come into no end of "oof." Are you surprised?'

Miss O'Shaughnessy was dressed in sea-green, and her draperies just then were too much like the colour of her skin to be becoming, She spoke after a second, in a constrained and hoarse voice:

'I wonder how Lord Ryde will like his son's marriage. As he's so ill, I am afraid it may upset him a good deal. Because though dear Kitty is of course *charming*, some of her relations are not quite—*quite*, don't you know? And there was that foolish rumour about her and an army doctor, you remember?'

Miss Malone passed the pair just then on her

bethrothed's arm. He was a tall man, undeniably handsome, in spite of a too-long neck and a head of a sugarloaf shape. His moustache was grey, and closely cropped, his eyes were prominent, and a little unsympathetic. His smile, although at first sight pleasant, expressed some consciousness of his own personal uprightness, and of his perfectly unblemished and prosperous career in the past, together with the least shade of contempt for other people who might happen to have stumbled or fallen on less easy roads. Miss Malone looked perfectly calm and unelated. Her soft cheeks were hardly flushed, her dark lashes did not rest upon them with a newly acquired sense of shyness; she only gazed with frank unconcern at her many friends and acquaintances. Her full red underlip did not quiver with emotion, but was merely parted from the curling upper one in a quiet smile. Kitty Malone was clever enough to ignore the envious or admiring glances that ran like lightnings over her slender figure—and apparently all-untouched by them, she walked up the whole length of the ball-room, with the confident and erect Captain Pelham at her side.

Now, sitting behind her barrier of pincushions and pen-wipers, of ponderous plush cushions and futile woollen mats, Miss O'Shaughnessy thought bitterly over this past scene. And the unconscious object of her gloomy meditation went on smiling amidst a tangle of ferns and blossoms, and giving a little girl directions as to how she was to take button-holes round the room and try to sell them. Mrs. Dowse, who presided over tea and buns, and weak claret and champagne cups, crossed over to the flower-stall for a minute.

'And are ye expectun Captain Pelham here to-day, my dear?'

'No, Mrs. Dowse, he has had to go over to England to see his father, who is ill. See, there is some one looking at your stall! They will pass on if you don't hurry back.'

Mrs. Dowse, fat and smiling, was behind her jugs and glasses in an instant.

'How I wish,' said Miss Kitty to one of her helpers, 'that some one of slight interest would come! We are selling for such a good object. Think of the poor soldiers having to leave their wives in a few days, and probably nearly all to be killed, or to die of fever in the horrible deserts! And those married without leave may be almost starving! Oh! Jenny, there *are* some soldiers coming in now! They are stopping at Nora O'Shaughnessy's stall. What use can an antimacassar or an illuminated text be to a soldier?'

'Well, they are not allowed to wear button-holes, and as they sail in four or five days, plants in pots won't be much use to them either.'

'Perhaps not. What a good-looking man that tall one is, with the three gold stripes on his sleeve, and the crimson sash.'

'Yes, a sergeant. And the fair man is a corporal. Oh! Kitty, how sad to think they'll probably be shot. How dreadful for you, dear, that Captain Pelham was given that staff appointment!'

'Ah! no, not quite that, I wish him to get on. I am immoderately ambitious, my dear Jenny.'

The sergeant and Miss O'Shaughnessy seemed meanwhile to be amused with one another. He laughed, showing a row of very white teeth, as he looked the young lady over from head to foot with a pair of reckless dark eyes. A couple of frugally-minded ladies came up just then to Miss Malone's stall, and after five minutes' quibbling, passed away in triumph with one little fern for sixpence, and a bunch of pinks for a penny. Kitty stood on a step, re-adjusting her flower-pots, her slender arms raised above her head, which was thrown a little backward. As she turned round something scarlet caught her eye. The young sergeant was standing facing her, tapping the edge of the stall lightly with his cane. His glance lingered on Kitty's slender form, taking in every detail of its grace and charm; the sky-blue dress with its broad sash, the shady black hat resting on her light brown hair. In the words of a far more famous sergeant he might well have said—'Thank you for the sight of such a beautiful face.' His eyes, however, told her as much, and the faintest pink flush overspread Miss Kitty's neck and her soft cheeks.

'I am afraid,' said the sergeant, taking up a large bouquet of shaded carnations, 'that you have fewer people at your sale than you expected?'

It was a commonplace remark, but Miss Malone started. The voice was that of a gentleman, and equally so the easy grace of his manner.

'Yes, indeed,' she answered. 'It's most disappointing. And one would have thought just now that so much sympathy would have been felt with the wives and children of our soldiers who are going to fight.'

The sergeant was leaning forward on the counter, his cane under one arm, his eyes fixed on the young girl's fair face. She, for her part, noted how exactly his uniform fitted his square shoulders and thin waist, how well his cap with its shining badge became him.

'Ah! I am afraid the inhabitants of this town don't feel any sorrow at our departure,' he said. 'We are not very much beloved here. For my part, I rejoice to get away.'

'Have you seen service before?'

'Oh, no. Now is my chance.' She fancied that he sighed a little.

'It's no use my offering you any of my lovely roses?' And the girl held up a large bunch on which the dew seemed hardly dry. The sergeant took them from her hand and smelt them.

'Alas! no. They are no good to me. I can't carry a nosegay about in the streets. Ah! there are some people coming to buy flowers. I am taking up your time?'

'Not in the least, I assure you.' And Kitty Malone actually blushed as she met once more the earnest gaze of those reckless dark eyes.

'The sale will go on this evening, won't it?'

'O, yes; it will all look much prettier lighted up. And there will be coloured lamps in the little garden at the back, where the gipsy sits, telling fortunes.'

'A fortune teller?—a genuine gipsy?'

'Well, no; I'm afraid I must confess that she is only a friend of mine dressed up. But she's very clever all the same. Why don't you have your coming fortune in this war foretold?'

'Ah!'—and he certainly did sigh this time, there was no mistake about it—'my fortune was told ever so long ago.'

'But think of what may yet happen to you in Egypt. O, I beg your pardon, Lady Celbridge. Which would you like of these lilies—these orange ones or the lovely variegated ones above?'

'Look at Kitty!' murmured Miss Nora O'Shaughnessy to her sister. 'What a flirt she is!

She even allowed that sergeant to stand and make eyes at her!'

'But we agreed just now that he was certainly a gentleman.'

'Yes, but it is so often the most hopeless scamps who enlist—men whose fathers will have nothing more to say to them.'

A band at the far end of the room began to play, and more people to troop in through the heavy doors. Mrs. Dowse was becoming crimson and hilarious over her urns and jugs of orange-ade. The sergeant stopped at her stall and drank some champagne-cup. Then he glanced over his shoulder at the flower-stall and the little blue figure among the blossoms, and began to pace slowly round the great hall, until a counter with some photographs attracted his attention. The owner, a lady who was a great admirer of Miss Malone, had fastened one of this young lady's portraits in a frame. The sergeant stopped.

'How much for this?' he asked carelessly.

'Oh, the photo of the lovely Miss Malone?'

'Exactly.'

'Well, ye can have ut for foive-and-six.'

The soldier paid the money, and the stall-keeper tied up the parcel.

'Put into a raffle, please, sergeant!' said a childish voice at his side.

He looked round and smiled pleasantly at a

little girl carrying a large cushion representing, in brilliant woolwork, Black-eyed Susan waving her lily hand to her departing William.

The sergeant laughed. 'I'll take two tickets, if you like.'

'And where shall I send it if you win?' asked the child.

'Colour-Sergeant Rhodes, . . . Barracks. But no, stay—it's no use to me; keep it for yourself if I win.'

When he had arrived at the end of the room the young soldier turned his head once more. He fancied that those large blue eyes behind the roses were actually watching him, and his thin brown cheeks grew a shade redder.

Towards seven o'clock the hall was ablaze with gas lamps, and, to the delight of the sellers, was at last thronged with townspeople. Miss Kitty had changed her blue dress for a cooler one of white muslin, and wore a fresh bunch of forget-me-nots pinned at her breast. By nine o'clock her stall bore the appearance of a forsaken garden. Only a few straggling plants, which had been earlier in the day relegated to the back rows, remained. Every bunch of carnations, and each neatly made button-hole, was sold. And Kitty thought that, considering the assiduous way in which she had worked, and how stifling was now the atmosphere of the room, she would allow herself a breath of fresh air in the garden. A few groups of dark figures stood on the gravel-path among the little twinkling red and green lights. The air was soft and cool, the sky of a dark velvety blue, with pale stars coming out. Round the little tent where the supposed gipsy sat, some dozen people were standing, and among them Kitty saw a tall, slight figure dressed in scarlet. One of the fairy lights illuminated the three gold stripes on his arm. As if owing to some magnetic influence the soldier turned his head sharply round as she advanced, and once more their eyes met, this time in a longer glance. The soft, languorous air crept round Kitty, rustling her white skirts, and lifting the curls on her forehead. She trembled a little. The sergeant came towards her, his brilliant figure standing out vividly against the sombre background of wall.

'So you've come back!' said Kitty Malone.

'It seems so. A few years ago I should not have thought that a sale and a sham gipsy would much amuse me; but as I am so soon leaving England—perhaps for always—I take rather a less *blasé* view of things.'

He came and stood beside her in the curious, uncertain light. The pale stars were not sparkling enough to lift the shadow off their faces; the fairy-lights threw odd little violet and green reflections upon her skirt and the red stripes on his trousers.

'Have you had your fortune told?'

'Not I. Nothing good is likely to happen to me ever again.'

'Why not? You might get a commission one of these days, and end as a general.'

They moved a little farther into the shadow.

'Only dreams!' he said. 'But I loathe talking of myself. Are you interested in this Egyptian business, or in anyone going out?'

They were almost in darkness now, so that if Kitty Malone had blushed the young sergeant would have been none the wiser.

'No.'

Kitty's thoughts travelled remorsefully for one instant beyond her companion, and she seemed to see a grave, commonplace face poised on an ungainly neck. But although she was about to make the most prosaic of marriages—to join her lot to that of an entirely respectable elder son of a rich peer—she had inherited with her Celtic blood a foolish craving for romance. Anyone as pretty as she was could have had no lack of lovers, but one and all had failed to bring her the excitement, the passionate desires, for which she sometimes longed. Here, in this dimly-lighted garden—so dully commonplace at the noonday, but glorified for an hour or so by the mysterious stars and the distant murmur of music

—she felt for once a strange thrill that was made up of both pleasure and grief.

'Miss Malone,' said the sergeant suddenly, 'you are extremely good to talk to me. For four—yes, five years no lady has said a word to me. I feel very much alone sometimes.'

'Indeed, I can understand that. But there are other men of your own class in your battalion with whom you can make friends?'

'Yes, now and then. But I know I have gone down hill. Not owing to the company of the men—no, I don't mean that, they are far better fellows, many of them, than I; but if one never sees a woman of one's own class one becomes coarser in tastes and pleasures, harder also, and more cynical. You have done me good, and I thank you, even if we should never meet again.'

'But we *may* meet some day. Anyhow, I will come and see your ship start.'

'Will you?' And he drew a little nearer to her. 'You are very kind to me.'

'How did you know my name?'

'I found it out. And I have your—no, never mind.'

'You must tell me who you are in return.'

'Sergeant Rhodes.' He paused a minute. 'That is the name I shall always be known by. Never by any other—never again.' His voice sank into a whisper.

'Shall we stroll round the gravel-walk, just once, Miss Malone?' he said, after a silence that seemed very painful to Kitty.

They walked slowly through the narrow garden, the distant music sounding in their ears—passionate, plaintive, tender. Then they came to a wooden bench, under a stunted tree. For an hour or more they sat there, learning so much, and yet, alas! so little about one another. A church clock sounded. The music stopped, and died away in a long-drawn sob. From a neighbouring garden a white cat leapt over the wall, the moon shining on its fur. The world seemed to have grown sadder and very silent. Kitty Malone sprang to her feet.

'O, how late it is! What will my uncle say, and my friends who were to have taken me home? Good-bye, Sergeant Rhodes.' She held out her little hand. The moonshine quivered on his pale handsome face—on the band of his cap and the scarlet and gold of his uniform. He looked at her long with the dark eyes which had grown graver now, and less reckless.

'Will you give me the bunch of forget-me-nots you wear in your dress?'

For a moment there flashed across Miss Kitty's romantic mind a memory of the beautiful American ballad telling of the lady who flung a rose down from her balcony as the column of war-worn men marched by. She trembled a little, but she took out the flowers, and he hid them away in his breast.

When Kitty came back alone, a few minutes later, the great hall was nearly deserted. Mrs. Dowse was yawning heavily over her emptied urns, and the O'Shaughnesseys had gone home. Miss Malone felt very much ashamed of herself, but, alas, more glad than penitent! In her joyous tremor she hardly realised that she had been behaving in a foolish, and, to say the least of it, a very unconventional way—in a manner which Lady Celbridge, her future husband's ideal of all that a lady should be, would have stigmatised as 'bad form'; she only knew that the triumphant happiness of this strange short evening was worth many an after hour of regret.

And perhaps into the heart of a man, reckless and dissipated enough, but a gentleman still, now lying awake in his narrow bed within blank barrack walls, she had brought some short glimpses of hope and retrieval—dim possibilities of redemption which, even if they should never blossom into flower, were yet as a handful of sparse verdure springing up in the desert of his soul.

CHAPTER II

'My dear Kitty, it is very foolish and emotional of you to wish to see the troop-ship start. You will probably be quite overcome, all the more so' — and here Captain Pelham patted his bethrothed's curly head—'as we—we, my darling, shall so soon also have to say good-bye to one another.'

Vincent could never entirely divest himself of a certain stiffness of manner, even when he was most genuinely moved, and his gestures, as bending over her, he stroked Kitty's hair, were, on this occasion, provokingly stilted and self-conscious.

Miss Malone looked him straight in the face, and smiled, half sadly.

'You needn't be afraid that I shall break down or disgrace you on this or any other occasion, Vincent. I really *do* wish to see the poor men sail. Lady Celbridge is going also.'

'That is quite a different thing, She has a young nephew bound for Egypt. Now there is no one in whom *you* are interested. Therefore I must continue to say I think it a little morbid of you, my dear Kitty.'

Captain Pelham straightened himself, stroked his moustache with both hands—a favourite habit of his—and allowed the subject to drop.

But it came about that two days afterwards Kitty Malone as usual got her way, and sitting on an outside car, with Lady Celbridge as her companion, drove to the station on a sunny, cloudless morning. After half an hour in the train, she sprang out, with flushed cheeks and shining eyes, and walked with her friend to the wharf.

Her glance fell on scores of soldiers in helmets and serge tunics, many of them with laughing, boyish faces, almost all trying to look as if they had at last attained the one desire of their hearts, and here and there on a woman with swollen eyes and lips tightly shut, to prevent any expression of emotion. She observed endless bales of luggage littered on the stones, horses about to be slung on board, careless and interested spectators getting in each other's way, talking, advising, gesticulating. Captain Vincent was already on the wharf, erect, self-satisfied, and well-dressed as usual. He advanced towards the two ladies.

'Well, Lady Celbridge, shall I go now and find your young man for you?'

'I wish you would! Dear boy, perhaps they would allow him to come to the hotel with me for a little while, and have a talk? He is my poor sister's only son, and I have been like a mother to him. Can I leave you here, dear Kitty? I thought I would go with kind Captain Pelham and find the boy, to save time. You have lots of friends, I know, here. Yes, there are the Staceys and the Egertons, I see; stay with them if you like.'

Miss Malone became dazzled by the glare of the sun, and by her constant efforts to discern a figure that was familiar to her among the red tunics. She knew that when the men were embarked, all would be over, and her last chance gone. She strained her eyes till the tears started into them. She found it very difficult to recognise people in the helmets that came so low over their foreheads. Suddenly, almost at her elbow two sergeants passed by. The taller one, with the smart, upright figure, was he at last, and she knew that he looked at her with the same lingering gaze that had attracted her before. But his glance left a different impression on her now. It seemed to imply reproach—was it even something stronger, disdain, contempt? Kitty Malone's cheeks grew pale as white roses when the young man, without making a sign of recognition, strode on towards the landing-place. Ah! he was a gentleman still, and he had never been introduced to her, she thought. He would not of course think it right to speak to her. But nevertheless her heart tightened strangely as she walked restlessly away to join her friends. Soon Vincent was back again, and at her side. She hardly heard his rather tedious explanations concerning the great ship lying as if asleep in the sun.

'Would you like to come on board, Kitty?'

Yes, she would. And, her heart still aching, she followed her betrothed across the gangway. Under the blazing rays she stood impassive, while Vincent introduced her to officers and others of his acquaintance, a half-smile flitting over her lips, as her eyes still wandered anxiously over the herd of scarlet figures. She saw that Sergeant Rhodes was standing some forty feet away, looking at her again. Kitty's cheeks burnt hotly, and her knees shook. She glanced at Captain Pelham's kind vacuous face, as with extended forefinger he laid down the law to a young veterinary surgeon. In a second she had approached the sergeant, and was holding out her little cold hand. He hesitated, raised his own to his helmet, hesitated again, and took it in his.

'I have come to say good-bye,' said Kitty in the shaking voice of a child who expects to be punished.

'Ah!'

'It was *really* to see you I came. I wanted to—O! it's so horrid and conventional to say, wish you luck, but you know what I mean!'

His eyes were merely reckless to-day. They had lost the softer look that had come into them a few evenings ago for just an hour.

'Thank you, Miss Malone. And *I* wish you all joy in the future, too. For myself, if you ever think of me enough to form a desire for me, let it only be this, that I may never come home or see you more.'

'O! What have I done?' Her voice was

drowned as the soldiers around her burst into a song. She started at the volume of sound.

> Should auld acquaintance be forgot—

The familiar and pathetic words sung by these full, boyish voices cut her to the heart.

> For auld lang syne, my dear,
> For auld lang syne . . .

And when she turned her head, Sergeant Rhodes was gone.

Again, as the dusk was closing in, and Kitty and Lady Celbridge hurried down to the wharf once more, she saw him. But he was not looking at her this time. He was talking to a comrade, and laughing so loud, that she could see his white teeth through the dim light.

When the moon came out, and the clouds moved slowly, like great black birds, over the funnels and masts, she saw him yet once again. The silver light made his helmet almost dazzling, and his face strange and blanched. As the great ship got slowly under way, the soldiers took their caps and helmets off, and cheered as they waved them. The pitiless moon smiled down upon the bare heads and boyish features, with the same callous stare with which she would watch them lying paler still in the deserts far away across the sea; where instead of the black clouds drifting to-night every moment farther off, evil winged creatures would then draw closer and closer to faces upturned and still. One young man, with gold stripes upon his sleeve, suddenly pressed forward and leant over the side of the ship, and amid the noise of deafening cheers and stifled sobs upon the shore, his eyes flashed a last message to a woman who watched him go, a message that could never have been uttered in words, even had the rushing seas not rolled between them.

CHAPTER III

MISS KITTY'S enemies—but, to do her justice, there were not many of these—acknowledged that she had wonderfully improved since the departure of Captain Pelham for Egypt. Lord and Lady Ryde, her future parents-in-law, wrote almost enthusiastically about her to other members of their family. Lord Ryde, whose hobbies were his own health and the results upon it of various patent medicines, thought her kindly and sympathetic. Lady Ryde had joined a strange sect, whose members tried to persuade her that her gout existed only in her own imagination, so with a bandaged foot, and three chalk-stones on one hand she sat meditating for hours, with Kitty at her side, urging the latter to support her in her strange belief; and her future daughter-in-law was always patient, and usually agreed with her to avoid argument.

Kitty's father, who had lived in London for years, and lost almost every characteristic of the race from which he had sprung, excepting a tendency to the display of outward emotion, had always considered his daughter faultless. But even *he* was sensible of her increased gentleness of manner, her more fully developed powers of sympathy, her patient consideration towards the shortcomings of others. She was very sad and silent sometimes, but that was of course only to be expected during Vincent's absence. Mr Malone was sincerely rejoiced to see how romantically in love she was with her future husband.

Kitty and her father left London towards the end of July, and installed themselves for a few months in a little river-side house with a rose-garden on one side and a tumble-down verandah on the other. She never forgot the expression that her father's face wore one evening after the late newspapers had arrived. She came in to find him standing by an open window, his hand shaking so that the sheets crackled, the tears running down his cheeks and the strangest triumphant smile lighting up his eyes.

He moved a few steps towards her, trembling still.

'Well, you're to marry a hero, Kitty, my darling! God bless him! See here! He handed the crumpled newspaper to his child, and, sitting down, buried his head in his hands.

Her face grew stiff and white as she read an enthusiastic account of the heroic conduct of a Staff-officer, Captain the Hon. Vincent Pelham, who, although himself wounded, had carried away in his arms a sergeant who had been more severely hit. The paragraph went on to say that this gallant action had been accomplished under a heavy fire, and that there was but little doubt that Captain Pelham would be recommended for the Victoria Cross which he had so thoroughly deserved.

The following morning 'The Times' brought more news to the river-side cottage — fuller details of the episode which was of so thrilling an interest to its occupants—and this time the name of the sergeant who had been dangerously wounded, and only saved from death by the valour of her lover, met Miss Malone's eyes. She had known by some strange instinct what it would be, and that evening, when she sat by her open window inhaling the perfume of a thousand roses, and listening to the gentle lapping of the water against the banks, she wrung her hands tightly together, and said, half aloud:

'Oh, why is one man to have all, and the other nothing—nothing till he dies! O God! Why may not I go to him, and tell him that whatever he is, whatever he has done—I care for him more than life itself! But he can never know, never know!'

CHAPTER IV

IN the early spring Captain and Mrs Vincent Pelham spent their honeymoon in a charming gabled house looking over wide downs and noble white cliffs in the Isle of Wight. This property belonged to an uncle of the bridegroom, and would in time, with many another good thing, become Vincent's own. The fresh breeze from the chalk slopes brought new roses to Kitty's cheeks, and they had been a little pale for some months past. People noted with admiration how much affected she had been at the time of her husband's illness, how proud she was of his success. And, without doubt, she did strive to make him happy. She struggled to overcome the phases of melancholy to which she was sometimes subject, to take an interest in many matters, dull and futile as they seemed to her, because they made up part of his life. And Vincent, if at times in his inmost heart he was a little mortified at her apparent indifference to the extreme good fortune that was hers, could not but acknowledge that she was sweeter and gentler than when he had first won her, and that she had for ever lost the slight tinge of flippancy that had sometimes annoyed him against his will. The pair had come into the garden one sunny evening after a long walk round a white precipice standing stern and gigantic out of a slate-coloured sea. Mr. Malone had arrived the day before to pay a visit to his children, and was in a sentimental and happy condition. He sat in a low chair, and smilingly awaited them as they came sauntering over the downs, their figures silhouetted against the purple of the western sky. At Mr. Malone's feet and all around him were large flower-beds of dazzling forget-me-nots, brighter than the distant sea, and the faint azure patches still lingering above to eastward. Kitty came up to her father, and, throwing one slender arm about his neck, kissed him lovingly.

'It is very nice to have you with us, papa dear.'

'And nicer still for me to be with my children. My little girl and her hero. Do you know, Vincent, dear boy, you have never shown me that little cross of yours, yet! Think of that!'

Captain Pelham began making holes in the gravel with his walking-stick. He was more refined in feeling than his father-in-law, and he had an almost morbid dislike to hearing allusions to his past acts of daring, especially when heralded by an exasperating smile of triumph from Mr. Malone. The latter would have been unable to appreciate such fine gradations of sentiment. He, for his part, delighted in recurring again and again to the war and its episodes, and in pestering Vincent with irrelevant questions. After tea had been drunk out of doors, the good old man wandered off to his favourite topic.

'And what has happened now, Vincent, my dear boy, to the sergeant, poor fellow, whose life you were so nobly the means of saving?'

Kitty looked away at the glimmering white cliffs and the expanse of placid sea.

'Oh, poor fellow, he's at Netley still; just across the water over there. I'm afraid he's done for. It's hard luck, because he's a gentleman, and might have got a commission one of these days.'

There was a short silence; then a blackbird chirped loudly and flew over the lawn into the bushes, while the crescent moon came slowly into view over the cliffs. Kitty spoke in a hard, dry voice.

'Couldn't we go, Vincent, one day over to Netley, and see that poor man?'

'My dear child, what earthly use would it be? I *did* see him once or twice, you know. And he's thoroughly well looked after. You certainly have a morbid taste for gloomy things.'

'But it might be kind; don't you think so, papa? I—I should so like to take him some flowers.'

'Well, my dear, surely Vincent knows best. It would upset you, no doubt, to see all those poor fellows, sick and wounded.'

The shadows crept silently over the garden, while the stars stole out over the ghostly cliffs, glimmering far away across the downs. Mr. Malone lighted his pipe, and Vincent began cheerfully to hum a few bars of an old song—

> 'When he who adores thee has left but the name
> Of his fault and his sorrows behind.'

He sang more than a little out of tune, and tapped the wooden bench cheerfully with his stick. And Kitty, with tearless eyes, and a drawn look about her mouth, listened as if in a dream.

CHAPTER V

THE soldier at the end of the ward had not spoken for twenty-four hours.

'Sinking fast,' said the doctor to a Sister, who wore a spotless white apron and scarlet cape over her shoulders, and who had just left the bedside.

'I fear so.' Sister MacDonald's sweet face

grew sad, and she sighed. She had felt very sorry for Colour-Sergeant Rhodes, and had nursed him tenderly during many dreary months of pain and discomfort. But she grieved less now that the indescribable blue shade was spreading at last over his face—that his eyes were shut, and the perspiration lying cold on his forehead. He was so lonely, and it was better that he should go, thought Sister MacDonald. Other men had friends to come and sit beside them—old and young women with tender and tearful eyes, and faithful hands to grasp theirs; but no one ever came to see Colour-Sergeant Rhodes.

When the post arrived that evening, the Sister found, rather to her surprise, that there was one letter at last for her favourite sergeant. She took it up to his bedside. He was breathing heavily, and his hand, when she touched it, was very clammy and cold.

'A letter for you,' she said in a low voice.

He lifted his eyelids a little, but made no other movement.

'Shall I open the cover and give you the letter?'

His lips moved, and she tore open the flap. It contained no writing after all—not a word of greeting or good-bye—only a bunch of forget-me-nots, so fresh and blue that they must have been very lately gathered. A pair of dark eyes opened wide, and were fixed earnestly upon the Sister. The soldier raised his cold fingers, and she put the little blue knot of flowers within them; and with quivering lips looked away from the dying man. He tried to hide the nosegay in the breast of his crumpled shirt. But his arm dropped upon the coverlet.

And when the last low sunrays smote the blank wall in front of Sergeant Rhodes' bed, he had passed where time and space exist not, and memory is, perhaps, by God's mercy, no longer the twin-sister of pain.

BAD AND WORTHLESS

CHAPTER I

A GALE was blowing from the north-west. It lashed a leaden sea into foam-crests, whistled under doors, rattled windows, and threatened lamp-posts and chimney-pots with destruction. It was a disconcerting wind to the few pedestrians who had braved it, and who were now mostly returning in a battered condition to their firesides. Among these were General Groser, and even he, stalwart and heavy as he was, found some difficulty in preserving his usually erect and pompous attitude as he walked. The gusts blew small fragments of ice off the asphalt into his eyes,—obliged him to hold on tightly to his hat, and ruffled his temper even more than his bristly white hair. The gale buffeted the little birds too, and they flew as if they were wounded. It certainly promised to be a wild night. Towards the sea, the road shone wet and white under a lurid dying sun. Over the grim-looking watery expanse, on which the outlines of a huge man-of-war were grayly defined, the sky was entirely black, with an under bar of orange, changing into lemon-colour. The distant island shores seemed dim and vague, as did the floating rack above them. General Groser pulled up his coat-collar and quickened his steps.

'We shall hear of disasters to-morrow,' he said aloud, looking at the ominous sea. Then he turned off into a side road where the lights of his substantial house glimmered a cheerful welcome. He found Mrs. Groser in the drawing-room, working at woollen comforters destined for a bazaar for 'waifs and strays.' She was a fat, colourless woman, whose red hair was beginning to turn gray. Her double chin rested on a large bow of magenta silk, and she wore easy 'spring-side' shoes.

'What an awful evening, George!' she said hardly looking up at him, intent on her crochet. The General coughed, stamped his feet, walked to the fire, whistled and blew on his cold fingers.

'There's a man outside,' pursued Mrs. Groser, 'in the back yard, waiting to see you. Madge has been talking to him, but you forbade her to give to beggars. He says he has been a soldier, and was in Burmah, and I don't know what besides.'

'There's simply no end to the scoundrels who come to my back-door.' said the General, gruffly. 'I've half a mind to give this one in charge to the police. But the worst of the police in this particular place is that you never by any chance see them when you want them. Where's the man? I'll just have a cup of hot tea, and then I'll go and speak to him, and send him about his business.'

The door opened to admit a maid of browbeaten aspect, bearing a smoking tray. The General ate a muffin and a half and drank two cups of tea. Just as he had finished, his niece Madge came in. She was an ugly girl, with a sweet and rather sad face.

'Uncle George!' she said, timidly.

'Yes, what is it?'

'Might I take a cup of tea to the poor man standing now in the yard? He looks so dreadfully thin and cold. I—I thought as it was all ready and hot, it wouldn't be any trouble; but if you don't like——'

The General looked furious.

'Tea be d——d!' he said.

'My dear George!' said Mrs. Groser, with her mouth full of bread and butter.

'You know my views, Madge!' pursued her uncle, still fiercely. 'I will *not*—be quiet, my dear Jane—I will *not* have these infernal men pestering me at the door of my house.' He seemed to swell as he spoke. 'The workhouse is the proper place for that sort of riff-raff. You know what your Uncle David told you the other day!'

Madge's mouth twitched. 'The workhouse is a long way from here,' she said, a little bitterly. 'The man looks quite starved and worn out already. I wish you would let me, *just for once*, give him my share of tea?'

'Hold your tongue!' said the General. 'I don't want to listen either to your advice, or your absurd wishes, my dear girl. Where's this fellow? I'll have a word with him!'

A shrunken figure was leaning up against the wall, near the back door; that of a rather undersized man, with a narrow chest and a hollow, white face.

'And what brings *you* here?' asked the General, rather sarcastically. 'If you've been a soldier, stand to attention, if you please!'

The man pulled himself together, and complied with the order.

'If you, sir, could just give me a copper, or a cup of tea, I'd be very grateful to you—I've not tasted a bit of breakfast or dinner.'

'I daresay! Where are your papers? Let's see what sort of character you bore when you were in the army!'

'Beg pardon, sir, I lost my papers three years since. But I can have a good character, sir, from them as knows me.'

The man spoke in a tired, apathetic voice, almost as if he were indifferent to the result of his words.

'Ah! that's what I thought! Lost your papers, have you? Look here—nobody gets a farthing or a crust from me if he can't give a better account of himself than *that*. You'—and the General here became almost eloquent—'you, and others like you, are the men who bring disgrace on Her Majesty's uniform. You're a curse to the noble British army. You loaf about the country, not even trying to get employment—getting drunk with any chance copper you may have, and pestering respectable people. Now be off!'

And General Groser pointed with a fat forefinger to the yard door. Madge looked compassionately at the man, although his aspect certainly was not prepossessing. His hair was suspiciously short, his face haggard, with a stubbly moustache; his eyes vacant, his whole bearing mean and despicable enough. But she was very sorry for him: all the more so as she, a poor relation whom the Grosers had adopted, did not dare to disobey them by giving him a penny. The man limped away through the green door, which slammed in the wind, out into the almost deserted road. For a minute he clung to the railing, for he felt dizzy and weak, and his feet were sore. Then he went slowly on.

General Groser, his face expressing the gratified consciousness of duty performed, returned to his drawing-room.

'You may be certain,' he said. rubbing his hands, 'my dear Madge, in spite of all your foolish would-be philanthropy, that that fellow's a real scamp! Discharged, I make no doubt, as a "bad and worthless character." And his physique! I ask you! Look what the army's coming to! Not thirty-two inches round the chest—a wretched, stooping, weak, deplorable object!'

The General threw his shoulders proudly back. He himself measured forty-one round the chest, and considerably more lower down. On one point, at least, he had been right in his conjectures. The character of the late Private O'Clery, who was a Londoner in spite of his Irish name, would not have borne minute inspection. He had undoubtedly given a considerable amount of trouble during his brief military career.

He had been frequently absent without leave, many times insubordinate and drunken. He had struck the Colour-Sergeant of his company in the face, for which offence he had been given one year's imprisonment with hard labour, and had been discharged from the service, as a 'bad and worthless character.'

But as he once remarked to a chaplain, who had vainly tried to influence him for good. 'Wot chance 'ave I ever 'ad?' An illegitimate child, cruelly treated by a drunken mother, brought up in a slum, and breathing a poisonous atmosphere of vice and degradation. A half-starved boy, who had learnt to drink and swear at the age when happier children are still under the care of nurses and tutors. A man with scarcely any education, no friends, no relations, no object in life. And now he was merely a beggar, footsore, and hungry, tramping along in the snow and the wild wind. Sometimes he had regretted just a little his complete failure to perform his duties as a soldier—that was when he recalled the warmth of the barrack-room, the hot dinners, the cheerful public-houses, the jests and laughter of his comrades. And it all seemed to him such years ago; though he was still a young man, scarcely thirty yet.

The gale rose higher and higher, and a few snowflakes fell. The air was so cold that O'Clery felt as if a knife were being scraped over his face, peeling off the skin. His hands were stiff, and he could hardly keep his battered hat on his head. He looked round to see if any one still lingered out of doors in this weather. Yes, there was an oldish lady with a long veil, carrying a basket, and hurrying down a side road. O'Clery followed her, and she shrank away from him, frightened at his haggard face. Then two young men, well dressed, with fur collars to their coats and cigars in their mouths, came along, walking very quickly. They belonged to a class of society which does not think it incumbent upon its members to respond to the remark of an unknown and inferior being, so they brushed silently past him, with their heads very much in the air. O'Clery rested for a few minutes by the door of a villa. He heard snatches of laughter, and bright young voices on the doorstep; and presently two girls, both young and pretty, came running down the path.

The ex-soldier came forward.

'Can you kindly oblige me with a copper, miss? I am almost starving.'

'I never give to tramps!' said the elder girl, looking at him suspiciously. Then O'Clery stared at them, and said something more coarse than flattering. His hollow, unmirthful laughter rang out through the cold air after their retreating footsteps. And he staggered wearily on again. Coming along the pavement he saw two more people, a man, neatly, but shabbily dressed, and a thin woman, pushing a perambulator. O'Clery stopped them. The woman looked sadly at his forlorn aspect.

'Pore fellow!' she said. And then she began fumbling in her pocket. She pulled out an orange, a bunch of keys, some sticking plaster, a photograph of a hideous baby, an enormous red handkerchief, and at last a halfpenny.

'That's all I've got with me!' she said. 'It's a bitter night for you to be tramping about. Where are you going to?'

'Gor-d knows!' said O'Clery, with a short

bitter laugh. And pocketing the coin, he pursued his way towards an outlying village. Arrived there, completely exhausted, he entered the public-house, spent his halfpenny in gin, and sat down awhile to rest. The landlord spoke to him.

'If you've been a soldier,' said he, 'I'd go up to the Fort. It ain't above three mile from here. P'raps the hawficers there might give you somethink.'

O'Clery thought the suggestion a hopeless one, but then the whole of his existence was hopeless. So he determined to walk up the hill to the Fort, and to reach it before nightfall. As he passed down the almost deserted village street, he met an old woman and some children hurrying home, and almost mechanically, he began to relate his misfortunes to them.

'Dear, dear!' said the old lady. 'That *is* a bad job! Nowhere to go to! And I've got a grandson in Burmah, a soldier, too, poor dear boy. Now young man, here's threepence for you—that's for Willie's sake. And mind you don't go for to spend it in beer!'

'No fear, Granny,' laughed O'Clery.

At the end of the village was a smaller and shabbier public-house. He staggered in through its swing door, and asked for three pennyworth of whisky. That would enable him, he thought, rather confusedly, to reach the Fort.

'Lor! wot a wind!' said the publican's wife, as a sudden gust rattled the glasses on the counter, and lifted the coloured prints from the wall. 'It's snowing fast, too,' she said, going to the window and looking out through the steaming panes.

O'Clery began to feel much more cheerful and stronger, and he did not notice the soreness of his feet so much. He only thought, philosophically, that if he got a little more money he would buy some boots that were not so hard and stiff as his present ones. The landlord wished him good-night, and he began his progress up the hill. He was surprised to see how fast it was snowing already. Some of the flakes were nearly as big as the palm of his hand. The wind was quite terrible. It came dashing down from the chalk hills in a mad rush, whirling the snow into his eyes, and whistling round his head with a loud and dreary music. He felt hopelessly tired, and the road grew every moment steeper. And always this plaintive rushing sound swelled higher and wilder. A solitary lamp-post groaned and shook like a figure of a man writhing in pain. Soon the air seemed all white, made up of nothing but huge feathers, drifting, flying, and whirling. Suddenly, from the side of the road, came another noise—unmistakably a human being weeping. O'Clery stopped to listen. It grew louder, and he went towards it. Then his foot stumbled against something and he fell forward.

'S'elp me!' he cried. 'It's a kid!'

A very small child, with a mop of yellow hair, had crept under the poor shelter given by a tall heap of stones. His clothes were already white with snow, and his little hands purple. Over his sailor hat the wet dropped upon his curls. He was sobbing bitterly.

'What's the matter, Johnny?' said O'Clery, kneeling down beside the forlorn little figure. But the child only cried louder.

'Oh come, shut up now! Lost yer mammy, 'ave yer?'

The child put his fragile arm round O'Clery's neck and drew closer to him.

'Where's mamma gone? Lost yer way, is that it?'

The child pointed vaguely down the hill. He was scarcely more than two years old; too young to make himself clearly understood. The darkness was coming on, not gradually, but as it were by leaps and bounds. Night itself was closing in, and ever the wicked wind blew more fiercely, drifting the snow in pure smooth heaps against the hedgerows.

'I'll tell you wot it is, Johnny, yer must come along with me. Hold on; put yer arms round my neck—so. There yer are!'

And O'Clery began to ascend the hill again;

very slowly and painfully this time, owing to his new burden. He was more than ever bent upon reaching the Fort before it should have become quite pitch-dark. He had been there once before, years ago, in the days when he too wore a uniform, and he remembered a great archway. He and the child would take shelter under that, perhaps. No one could drive a dog away on such a night. The child's yellow head was beginning to shake up and down over O'Clery's shoulder. He was fast asleep, and like the man who carried him, very numb and weary.

'Damn this hold Fort!' said the soldier. 'We don't seem to get no nearer. By ——.' He had caught his foot in something, a large stone probably, and uttering a variety of expletives it were better not to record, he fell heavily down, sinking into the snow. The child woke up and screamed.

'Stop that row!' said O'Clery, angrily, for he was conscious of a sharp pain in his foot and ankle. He struggled to rise, but vainly. And the little boy began to whimper and moan plaintively. Despairingly, O'Clery made one more effort, unavailing, like the last.

'The blasted bone must 'ave got broke,' he said. Then he crawled on his knees, still carefully holding the child. But he was beginning to feel a deathly sickness stealing over him. It was true that he had not tasted a mouthful of solid food for many hours; in fact, for days past his poor shrunken body had been quite insufficiently nourished. His heart sank within him. He knew that he could never reach the Fort that night, and that not a soul would be out in this cruel weather. He shouted, but his voice sounded strange and weak. Then, from a long way off a familiar sound fell on his ear. A bugle. It was the call of the 'First Post.'

'It's —— hard luck for the kid,' murmured O'Clery. He sat down now in the snow, the pain in his foot increasing till it became almost agony. The child moved his arm, and said something that sounded like 'To—de: 'ands 'urt!'

'I 'spect yer *are* cold, Johnny. Give us yer 'ands and I'll rub 'em up a bit.' And the ex-soldier tried to chafe the small icy fingers out of their state of numbness. The moments seemed to drag very slowly by. And the snow was certainly getting thicker . . . and higher. . . . Far off, over the dreary white landscape came the echo of another bugle at last. A longer call. The 'Last Post.' And the child was now sound asleep. Then a really brilliant thought struck the fuddled brain of O'Clery. With stiff fingers he loosened the little boy's grasp, and laid him down for a moment. After that he took off his tattered coat and waistcoat, and carefully wrapped them round the child. They completely enveloped his tiny figure. Then, with a still greater effort, for his foot was beginning to swell, O'Clery drew off his ragged boots and stockings. His upper garments had been filthy enough, but they were clean when compared with his patched hose. Mrs. Groser and her lady friends would have withdrawn in horror from any contact with garments in such a condition. But of this the child knew nothing. And O'Clery drew the dirty stockings right over his little shoes and legs. Then he put on his own boots again. The boy nestled closer into his arms, unknowing now that the world was dark and cruelly cold. Once again a bugle sounded. This time it was 'Lights out.'

And the ex-soldier's head dropped lower and lower, till it rested motionless on his pillow of snow.

CHAPTER II

THE dawn, spreading a pure pink glow over the landscape, had not long broken when two figures, those of a man and a woman, came up the hill, their feet leaving large patches upon the untrodden white surface. They looked anxiously and inquiringly from side to side.

"'E must have come all the way up from the village, bless 'is 'eart,' said the woman.

'Well, 'e won't be alive if 'e come much more fur than this,' answered the man, calmly.

Both speakers obviously belonged to the vagrant class, who tramp from hamlet to hamlet, mending kettles and pans, and living from hand to mouth as they go. The woman had a not unkindly face, and wore a crape hat lurching over to one side. Both she and the man had been dead drunk the evening before, and had not discovered that they had left the child behind until they were completely incapable of going to seek him.

Suddenly Mr. Higgs—such was the travelling tinker's name—stopped dead short, uttering a succession of oaths. After which he shouted, 'See 'ere, Eliza!'

The lady who, temporarily at least, bore the title of Mrs. Higgs, came up panting, very red in the face.

'See 'ere!' cried Mr. Higgs, again.

The snow had drifted into a high, spotless hillock against a five-barred gate and a tall hedgerow. Below the ridge was seen the recumbent figure of a man, or, to be more exact, a portion of such a figure, embedded in snow. Lying right across the man's body was what appeared to be a bundle of rags and motley garments, surmounted by a bush of golden hair.

'That's 'im, by —!' exclaimed Mrs. Higgs. 'My beauty! 'ere's mamma!'

In a moment she was kneeling beside the child, who was either asleep or insensible.

'Eliza!' said the man, in a voice which showed him to be not entirely unmoved. 'Don't yer go on a-hollering and a-bellering! It don't foller, old girl, that 'e's 'opped the twig.'

And he took up the child and undid the wrappings—filthy, ragged garments—that enveloped him.

'I see 'im move!' said Mr. Higgs, triumphantly. ''E winked 'is hy! We'll take 'im to the pub at once, Eliza, and there ain't any reason, as I can see, why these ere togs shouldn't go with 'im. The late owner'll never want them no more.' And he glanced at the perfectly rigid figure that lay in the snow.

'Pore chap, *'ee'll* not move again, or want clothes, that's a sure thing,' said Eliza. And she scraped away the snow and laid her red hand on the motionless heart of that bad and worthless character, the late Private O'Clery.

'Well, Billy, my man,' said Mr. Higgs, 'so we've found yer again. And a precious 'unt we've 'ad of it. And yer shall keep yer new *trooso!*' he added, with a grim laugh.

The yellow-haired boy opened his eyes, cried, smiled, and rubbed his face with his little blue fingers.

''E shall have a drop of something warm when we get to the next pub,' said Eliza, encouragingly. And the tramps walked on, more quickly this time, just turning back to glance again at the figure lying so still by the hedge.

A little later on, when the village began to wake into life, there was bustle and stir in the Fort above on the hill. Privates Varley and Maddox were missing, absent all night without leave.

The Adjutant looked grave.

'It's awful weather for men to have been out,' he said. 'Especially when they've lately come from such a hot climate as Mandalay.'

The sun rose higher, melting some of the snow. Children, warmly wrapped up, got ready for school. And a fatigue-party, consisting of a corporal and six men, came with smart steps past the hedgerow and the gate where O'Clery's body lay.

'Hold hard there!' said the corporal, sharply.

The soldiers advanced towards the recumbent figure. Its shabby boots—the man wore no stockings—stuck out aimlessly. His head was thrown backwards, displaying a scraggy neck, rising out of a torn and dirty shirt. He wore neither coat nor waistcoat. His stiff hands, which looked quite yellow in the pure snow, were tightly clenched. The corporal looked at him with mingled compassion and disapproval. He was a very smart, clean, respectable man a credit to his regiment, but a little severe in his judgments.

'The man's been and pawned his clothes for drink. That's clear!' said he, with decision. 'And that's what many people—soldiers, too, I'm sorry to say—come to. Lift him up, Barnes, and see if anything can be done for him!'

'He's quite dead, corporal,' said Private Barnes, looking rather scared. 'He's been a soldier, too,' he added to one of his comrades. 'See the tattooing up his arm.'

'A soldier, and pawned his last clothes for drink!' repeated the corporal, decisively. 'That sort of man's a disgrace. But he's been the sufferer, there's no doubt of that.'

Then they lifted the ghastly body, and bore it to the police-station.

That morning the bodies of Privates Varley and Maddox were also found in their snow graves—victims of the bitter night just passed. And, as they, poor fellows, deserved, they were buried surrounded by comrades, and the band played a grand funeral march, which in its earlier chords seems to tell of the throbbing of pain and the voices of anguish, and in its close to peal forth a rapture of triumphant joy. On the following Sunday the chaplain preached, in touching accents, of the unforeseen death of these two gallant soldiers, and tears not a few were shed for them in their far-away homes.

But no one came to O'Clery's funeral, and not a soul, excepting the gravedigger, remembered the place where his half-starved body was laid.

* * * * *

It was two days after the storm. There were still a few scarlet geraniums left in General Groser's front garden, dilapidated little blossoms, but shining crimson above thin layers of snow. Madge stood on the lower balcony feeding the birds that looked abnormally large and black against a white background. She came into the dining-room just as the General and Mrs. Groser, and the brother of the latter, had taken their places at the table. The clergyman said grace, in which he dwelt, at some length, on the imperative duty of administering to the wants of the poorer brethren. Then he helped himself to a large and succulent mutton-chop. He wore a rather frayed white tie and straggling whiskers. It was his custom to walk up occasionally from his vicarage to breakfast with his brother, saying that early rising, and a brisk walk before food, were good preventives of self indulgence. Madge, for her part, wondered if the real inducement was the superior quality of the cooking to be found at the General's table, and then blamed herself for judging uncharitably.

On this particular morning, the host was in a

very conversational mood. Spreading out a damp copy of the daily paper, he read aloud several extracts, interspersed with a running commentary of platitudes and moral sentiments.

'Dear, dear, a severe wreck on the Yorkshire coast! Shocking, David, is it not, to think of all those poor creatures hurled into eternity at a moment's notice!'

'Yes, and doubtless many totally unprepared to go!' remarked Mrs. Groser, placidly, spearing a sausage with her fork.

'Ah! truly a terrible thought!' remarked the Rev. David with his mouth full. 'Our naval and military men lead, I fear, not unfrequently sadly reckless and immoral lives.'

'But they have so often such good hearts, and people do all they can to put temptations in their way!' Madge said, speaking very quickly and shyly.

The Rev. David looked at her with pity and disapproval. He mentally divided the world with a hard equatorial line into two hemispheres, one thickly populated with an abundance of goats, the other sparsely, containing but a few sheep. He was not yet quite decided in mind to which section Madge belonged. He feared that it might be the former, but as he rather disliked her, his uncertainty predominated over his grief at the possibility.

'Ha!' said the General, spreading out his

newspaper, and tapping it. 'Ha! How right I was, if this is the same fellow!' He read aloud—'Among other casualties resulting from the severe snowstorm, besides the many disastrous ones already related, we may record the discovery by some soldiers from Fort . . ., of the dead body of a man, presumably formerly in the army, which was found embedded in the drifts, not a mile from the above-mentioned fort. Life had been extinct some hours, and it is supposed that the unfortunate deceased had pawned most of his garments for drink, as he was found in a semi-nude condition. He had doubtless fallen down in a heavy stupor, owing to the influence of alcohol, and met his death in the melancholy manner described.'

'I've a presentiment,' continued the General, triumphantly, 'that this will prove to be the same scoundrel who came to my back door! For he took the road leading up towards the Fort, you remember? Pawned his clothes for drink! What a deplorable and disgusting end!'

'But if——,' began Madge.

'My dear,' said Mrs. Groser, 'Do not, I beg of you, argue with your uncle! He must be the best judge. He shows great insight into character by turning away the undeserving.'

'Exactly!' and the General rubbed his hands. 'They take the bread out of the mouths of honest people.'

BAD AND WORTHLESS 51

'Ah!' sighed the Rev. David. 'They are fit neither for the land, nor for the dunghill, so men cast them out.'

He was so pleased with this quotation that he repeated it twice over.

Madge pushed back her chair, and went over to the window. Through a mist that overspread her eyes she saw the melting snow, the ragged red blossoms, the hungry birds. The sun was quite bright now, shining upon a glittering sea, and the giant outlines of the ship that had been unable as yet to leave her harbour owing to the great gale. Cheerful people came out of their houses, hurried down the asphalt walk towards the town; and the sound of a distant military band fell upon Madge's ear. She thought the while of the starving, shrunken man at the back gate, and pictured him lying dead and lonely up on the far white hills.

The General rose from his chair, walked to the fire, and stretched his hands cheerfully over the blaze. Then he rang the bell. The browbeaten maid responded to his summons.

'We are ready for prayers,' said he.

A SUCCESSFUL INTRUSION

CHAPTER I

MOST people who have spent the 'mother of months,' or a part even of May, in Rome, must look back with a tender regret to visions of blue skies, to past hours of continual sunshine and splendour. They will recall, as in a dazzling dream, days when they left the ruins and the cool churches of the city to wander among garlands of briar-roses and vetches, through myriads of blossoms, gold and violet, pink and snow-white. In the kingdom of fancy they will travel once more over the undulations of the green Campagna, they will listen to the quivering song of the lark at morning, and to the vespers of the nightingale. They will even smell again—so vivid is the remembrance of these dead delights—the odours of the orange-blossoms that made the breezes sweet on those wonderful starlit nights of 'delicate-footed May,' long ago.

In one of the dull, great Bayswater houses that overlook Kensington Gardens, there sits to-day a pale, sad-eyed little governess, who has long passed her first youth, and who looks out of her window sometimes on a warm spring evening, dreaming somewhat in this fashion. The visions pass, but they make a bright interlude in her life spent among maps and inkstained books, and varied only by monotonous walks down dust-laden roads and drab-coloured streets.

A good many years ago, on one of the latter days of April, a larger party than usual was assembled at the six o'clock *table d'hôte*, in the dining-room of one of the most popular hotels in Rome. It was unpleasantly hot even in this lofty apartment, although the head waiter had obligingly turned out some of the gas-burners at the request of a heated English clergyman, who wore spectacles and a limp collar and white tie. There was as usual a jingle of knives and forks and clatter of dishes, but at the end of the long table, where the clergyman was sitting, there was also a quite unwonted buzz of mirth and cheerful conversation. Even the prim old maid of the party, Miss Hertz, was shaken with unmusical laughter, and a stern ecclesiastic—not the one who wore spectacles, but an older and much more severe person—was this evening affable and unbending.

From the way that the guests at this end of the table, who were, one and all, obviously British, addressed each other jocosely across the table, and exchanged amused glances, it was obvious that they must be old acquaintances, for it is well known that John Bull and his wife, when on tour—to use the colloquial expression—always keep themselves to themselves. This pleasant gathering of worthy English men and women had been all brought together to see the sights of Rome, and other Italian cities, under the protecting wing of the Rev. Andrew Furber, the little clergyman in spectacles. Once or twice a year he personally conducted some such party as this to different parts of Europe. To do him justice, it was no sordid love of gain that had suggested to him the advantage of arranging these little journeys. It was from a most genuine and philanthropic desire to interest and amuse his hard-worked brother clergy, their female relations, and other humble people who could not have afforded the luxury on less economical principles. The Rev. Andrew, after long experience and study, had become an adept in the art of reducing all expenses to a minimum, and as a larger number of travellers joined his party every succeeding year, so much the more moderate did the charges become. This year saw the epoch of his greatest triumph, and the good little man's face wore an almost unceasing smile of gratification. No less than eighteen precious souls had been all agog to join him, and there they were, every mother's son and daughter of them, in good health and spirits, safely arrived at the crowning point of the journey—the end and aim of their pilgrimage—the Eternal City itself.

By Mr. Furber's scheme one fortnight was to be devoted to the exploration of the glories and beauties of Rome. In his circular, which had been issued for months past throughout the British Isles in halfpenny wrappers, he had announced that one of the chief attractions of the Italian tour would be the lectures, to be given throughout its course by the Rev. Augustine Gadsden, of Balliol College; and that another would be the opportunity of learning sketching from the promising artist in water-colours, Mr. MacClymont of Inverness.

On this particular hot evening the attention of all the ladies, and of several of the men, who belonged to Mr. Furber's party, was centred round a stranger who, by some error, had been piloted by Fritz, the head waiter, to a seat adjoining Mrs. Gadsden's. That lady had at first frowned, rustled her skirts, demurred a little, coughed, and looked plaintively at Mr. Furber and sternly at Fritz. But after a few minutes a change stole over her face. The stranger appeared so happily unconscious that he was intruding where he was not wanted; his manners and voice were so irresistibly charming, that they would have softened the harshness of John Knox himself. And, moreover, this young man's personal attractions were as striking as were the grace and dignity of his bearing. He had a tall figure and a small head set upon broad shoulders, flashing eyes which might have been either dark-brown or deep-grey, hair which, in spite of being cut as close as possible had an attractive wave about it, a straight nose, and delicately-cut lips. He was clean shaven, and beneath his clear dark skin there was a tinge of red which imparted an air of vigour and freshness to his face. But it was when he smiled that Mrs. Gadsden succumbed entirely to his fascinating personality. Her husband, the Rev. Augustine, had spent the whole proceeds of two elaborate and learned articles upon the 'Hall of the Muses' in fees to an American dentist; but the work of this scientist could by no means rival what nature alone had done for this very agreeable young man.

'It has just occurred to me,' he was saying, 'that you are all thinking that I have no business here at all. Nay, I confess it—the worthy Fritz did offer me a seat at the other end of this table, but I am so solitary here, and the sight of all your bright faces was a great temptation to me! I know Mr. Furber well by reputation, and in fact have met some of his relations in England, and I have often heard of the success of his charming tours. I can't say I wonder at it. This time he seems to have been particularly happy in his choice of friends and fellow-travellers.'

He had dropped his voice just a little, and glanced, for a half-second only, at Mrs. Gadsden's thin face—one which had been pretty some ten years ago, and which bore traces of good looks still, although her mouth had a discontented expression, and her skin was sallow by the light of day.

The old maid, Miss Hertz, upon whose fat hands many rings sparkled, now turned her attention to the newcomer.

'You are a stranger in Rome, I presume?' she asked in a stuffy voice. Miss Hertz had no need to join Mr. Furber's party for reasons of economy; but, like many other wealthy people, she knew the value of a sixpence, and generally got it.

'I only arrived yesterday. But I already know Rome very well.'

'What a delightful voice he has!' murmured Mrs. Furber to her neighbour, a girl with large brown eyes, 'such a curiously attractive intonation!'

The young lady addressed softly agreed, and looked shyly at the stranger. Then she bent her gaze downward upon her plate.

Miss Hertz had entered into a lively conversation with him across the table. She was so engrossed that she had forgotten to keep a tight hold upon her knife and fork, which were now undergoing a perfunctory dab with a napkin in an adjoining recess.

'Ah, the late ambassador was a friend of yours! Of course it must be of great advantage to know the diplomatic circle here.'

'I have a letter to our present one,' said the stranger, smiling, 'but I don't think I shall avail myself of it. I don't care to go in for society; I shall merely wander a little about my old haunts, and then turn my steps slowly homewards.'

The Rev. Augustine Gadsden began talking very loud. Perhaps he also wished to attract the attention of this obviously distinguished young man.

'We will make our way to some of the tombs to-morrow,' said he. 'You, my dear Furber, no doubt recall the lines, familiar to every schoolboy—

'"Quantos ille virum magnum Mavortis ad urbem
  Campus agit genitus . . ."'

'Ahem!—ah! Strange; I know it as well as my own name——'

'"*Vel quæ, Tiberine vidibis,*" etc., etc.,' interrupted the dark-eyed stranger courteously, with a smile.

'To be sure, to be sure!—what was I thinking of? Thank you, sir,' said the Rev. Augustine, only half-pleased at the interruption.

'A classical scholar, too!' murmured Mrs. Furber to the brown-eyed girl.

Mr. Gadsden resumed his monotonous lecture upon the tombs, until gently but firmly checked by Mr. Furber.

'I propose,' said the latter deferentially, and beaming at his friends through his spectacles, 'that we should make up two parties to-morrow —one, the less learned one,' and Mr. Furber smiled at the ladies, 'to see the Protestant cemetery, the other to listen to Mr. Gadsden's most interesting and instructive discourse in the Catacombs. After dinner I will, if you are so minded, take pencil and paper, and make a list of the members of our respective parties. What say you, Miss Routledge?'

The girl to whom he spoke lifted her lovely eyes again.

She had a provoking way of keeping them downbent, thought the stranger.

'I think it would be an excellent plan, Mr. Furber. I am not one of the learned ones, though, I am afraid,' she said.

As he was a middle-aged, married clergyman, Mr. Furber could, without any indiscretion, playfully pat Miss Routledge on her pretty little head.

'Well, my child, I've half a mind to join you,' he said. 'And I'm sure my wife will. And what says dear Mrs. Gadsden? and our kind Miss Hertz? Shall we go and mourn over the remains of our two immortal poets, or shall we——'

'My love, dinner is over,' said Mrs. Furber.

'And good business too,' yawned the person, who had been sitting on the other side of Miss Routledge—an overgrown boy, with a muddy complexion. He was the son of the Very Rev. the Dean of ——, who had intrusted him to Mr. Furber's care in the hope that he would pick up more information on this tour than he had ever gained from former studies.

'This is the filthiest grub I ever swallowed,' continued the young man, as he noisily pushed back his chair. 'And there isn't such a thing as a clean fork inside these four blessed walls. Look at old Hertz making eyes at that chap with the clean-shaven face. What luck for him! She's got fifteen thou. a year, if she's a penny. I suppose that's why she travels with Furber third-class, and makes tea and toast on the cheap in her bedroom.'

The party of English travellers entered the *salon*, which contained polished floors, enormous mirrors, in which Mrs. Furber thoughtfully stared at her flushed face, a selection of newspapers fastened on sticks, and carefully arranged bouquets of artificial flowers. The young stranger who had joined them at dinner followed them into the sitting-room, and introduced himself to Mr. Furber.

'My name is Villiers Oswald,' he said, 'and I have often heard of you from my aunt, Lady Pitcairn.'

Mr. Furber looked puzzled.

'O, you may have forgotten her; but she was at S. Moritz one year when you took the duty there, and she was enormously struck by your preaching. In fact, I remember hearing her quote sentence after sentence from your sermons.'

Good Mr. Furber's face shone.

'It is very amiable of Lady Pitcairn to think so well of me, and of you, my dear sir, to tell me,' he said simply.

'I wonder if I might, without appearing very pushing, offer to join one of your parties tomorrow?' said the young man, half shyly. 'I am a little dull here just now, because my friend, who was to have joined me, changed his plans. And I cannot help being charmed by the *bonhomie* of many of your travellers. You all seem like one happy family, and I feel I am the poor outcast at the gates.'

'Nothing could please us more, I'm sure, than to have you as an addition to our little party,' cried Mr. Furber with enthusiasm, looking towards the round table where Mr.

and Mrs. Gadsden and Miss Hertz sat, the latter engrossed in the study of an old paper of fashion-plates. The Rev. Augustine was furtively fingering the outside only of a new novel by Zola.

'People should not leave such books as this on the table of a respectable hotel,' he remarked, with compressed lips. 'One's wife or one's daughter may in all innocence open it, and their eyes may drink in pollution. This realistic school——'

'I, for one, fail to see why this branch of literature alone should be called by that epithet,' said Mr. Oswald. 'Must we only apply that word to all the revolting things in nature? Surely it is as realistic to describe a shining trout-stream as to dilate upon the contents of a sewer? But you are quite right. Such books ought not to be left where ladies can see them.'

Mr. Oswald took up the obnoxious volume and put it under his arm. It is possible that he may have sat up during part of the night with the novel as a companion, but of this Mr. Gadsden could know nothing.

Mr. Oswald bent over the wife of this gentleman, and admired the work with which she seemed engrossed.

'It is for a bazaar for reformed inebriates,' said that lady.

'What a good object!' cried Mr. Oswald. 'I am for giving everybody, however depraved, a chance. My aunt, Lady Pitcairn, has taken great interest in that question. Mrs. Gadsden, I am only a useless man—I can't paint, I can't do embroidery; but may I give you my mite towards such an excellent cause? Now, before I forget it.'

He looked earnestly at Mrs. Gadsden.

'It's too, too kind, but I don't like——' she murmured. 'On such a short acquaintance—'

Mr. Oswald smiled, and produced a sovereign from his pocket.

'You see, you can be very persuasive, although you haven't begged in words, Mrs. Gadsden,' he said; but in such a low voice, that the Rev. Augustine did not hear him.

Mrs. Gadsden actually blushed a little, and the colour that came into her sallow cheeks made her pretty for a moment.

Villiers Oswald looked at her with a long, sympathetic gaze. He guessed that she was rather sad, and misunderstood and lonely, for he added very gently, and in a still more subdued and gentle voice—

'I suppose you indulge in many dreams over your work, Mrs. Gadsden, as we all of us do when our hands move mechanically and our brains are restless and weary?'

'Perhaps it is wiser not to dream,' said Mrs. Gadsden darkly. And she fancied that Mr. Oswald sighed. He rose, and moved slowly across the shiny floor of the *salon* to where little Miss Routledge was sitting, attended by the Dean's unattractive son.

'Well, you are not at work, at any rate, either of you,' said Mr. Oswald. 'There is nothing so really delicious in the world, let wise people say what they like, as to sit perfectly still, in a half-comatose state, and not even to bother one's self to think.'

'I should never be happy for a moment if I were idle,' said Miss Simpson, a thin girl with light eyes and a demure smile. Miss Simpson was hemming a large under-garment by the light of a lamp that stood on an adjoining table.

'Well, anyhow my day for dawdling will soon be over,' remarked Miss Routledge, sighing, and stretching her slight arms over her head. 'Three weeks more, and I too shall be numbered among the toilers of the earth, Miss Simpson. You wouldn't grudge me my present little spell of delightful laziness under those circumstances, would you?'

Mr. Oswald drew up a spindle-legged chair near to the one occupied by Miss Routledge, and said in his most sympathetic tones—

'And what, Miss Routledge, if it is not

impertinent of me to ask, may be the particular branch of work that you have chosen to take up? I should guess it to be art in some form—music, perhaps, painting more likely?'

Violet Routledge blushed. 'I do paint a little, but not well enough to make a career of it,' she answered, rather sadly. 'No, I am going to be nothing more romantic than a governess. I shall live in Bayswater, and teach tiresome children for seven hours a day, and walk out with them for two. Now and then I shall be taken to a bazaar as a great treat; once or twice a year I may have a week's holiday. And so on, and so on, till—till I grow quite old, I suppose, and don't wish for treats any more.'

'*You* a governess!' said Mr. Oswald. Into those three words he threw a vast amount of meaning. They said as plainly as possible, 'The idea is unendurable. You are much too young and lovely to throw yourself away like that.'

'Ah! but what am I to do? I have no friends but one old uncle, and he has very kindly sent me away on this tour, so that I may have a last taste of liberty. It is very dear of him, and I am sure his twenty pounds could not have been more delightfully spent.'

'It is marvellous how Mr. Furber can do everything so well on such a small sum,' observed Mr. Oswald thoughtfully. 'He told me that you have been to Genoa and Pisa, and I don't know where besides. But you must really get him to prolong your stay in Rome a little. I am sure that none of the party could grudge a very trifling increase of cost to see more of this divine place—a fortnight is impossibly short for Rome.'

'I am glad *you* think Furber does things well,' growled young Mr. Pepys, the dean's son, who had no intention of being left out of the conversation. 'If you happen to like dirty third-class carriages, and greasy cooking, and sour wine, and putrid syphons, *I* don't. That's the sort of thing we've been having, on and off.'

'O Mr. Pepys!' expostulated the refined Miss Simpson from her far corner. 'What *have* we to complain of? Perhaps the eggs yesterday were a *little*——'

'Not exactly bad, but "eggs that had seen trouble," as the Yankee observed?' said Mr. Oswald, inquiringly.

'That's not a new joke!' said Mr. Pepys with a snort. 'All *I* say is, that this is the last time, and I shall tell my governor so, that I come out of England on a fool's errand.'

'I should have thought that the company would have made up for any little drawbacks such as those you mention,' and Mr. Oswald glanced at Miss Routledge, with an innocent air, from under his long eyelashes. 'Tell me some more about your fellow-travellers,' he continued, addressing himself entirely to the pretty young lady. Young Pepys scowled at them both, rose, and walked away to the other side of the *salon*. Miss Simpson followed him, waving her unfinished nightdress.

'Well,' said Violet Routledge, 'there are the Gadsdens! He is very learned and clever, and gives lectures. He will do so to-morrow.'

'Oh! Not at the Protestant cemetery?'

'No, I think he will lecture for the other party. Then there is a Miss Hertz. She is enormously rich.'

'Oh, enormously rich, is she? I noticed that her rings were lovely.'

'Yes, she keeps them under her pillow with her money-box. She takes them all off whenever we go out, and then she wears grey cotton gloves. Isn't it funny for anybody so rich to wear grey cotton gloves!'

'And who is the young man with the stringy hair and the projecting teeth who is talking to her—is he economical too? For I see that he wears a flannel shirt, although the weather is by no means chilly.'

'Oh, that is Sir Arthur Cracroft! He *is*

stingy, I believe, because I have noticed that he always fights about giving tips to the waiter. He collects what he calls *curios*. He has got all sorts of lovely boxes, and some old enamels and watches and snuff-boxes, some of which he has picked up since he has been on this tour.'

'He doesn't keep them under his pillow, I suppose?'

'No, in an old hair trunk. His luggage is no smarter than his clothes. Well, let me see —that is Miss Simpson's brother—he is going to be a barrister.'

'Ah! I see—the brother of that typical English miss, *qui fait la bouche en cœur*.' Mr. Oswald spoke with a perfect French accent. 'And that cheerful boy with the singularly affable manners—who is he? He does not seem to enjoy himself.'

'I think he would like—well—you see, a more lively set of people. He wanted to play cards in the train, but that old lady who belongs to our party—the one with the grey curls—she is a strict French Protestant, and she told Mr. Furber that a *pasteur évangélique* should not countenance such things.'

'Ah! the youth likes cards? So do I, just a quiet game of bézique—or piquet now and then. But, of course, not for money. Ah! there is good Mr. Furber going round with his pencil and paper. He is coming to ask whether you will wander among the Catacombs with that well-informed old parson, or whether you will stay aboveground with—' and he lowered his voice a little—'myself, perhaps, amongst other people? For I too shall visit the cemetery, I think, to-morrow.'

Mr. Furber, his face one broad smile, came towards them.

'Well, my dear Miss Violet,—weather permitting—and if we are all spared—where will you go to-morrow?'

'I think I should like to see the cemetery,' said that young lady demurely.

'And I would also,' said Mr. Oswald, 'if you will allow me. The poet Shelley, by the way, was a distant connection of my family, on my mother's side.'

Mrs. Gadsden joined the group, and Mr. Furber beamed on her also through his spectacles.

'You, of course, my dear lady, would not wish to miss your husband's most interesting address in the Catacombs?'

Mrs. Gadsden's sallow face became flushed, and she frowned a little.

'Thank you, I will go to the cemetery,' she said; and her voice was not exactly pleasant.

CHAPTER II

Though the sun in the streets was scorching, and there was hardly a breeze stirring, the quiet graveyard lying below the great Roman walls was fresh and green. Some ten people, most of them wearing dusty clothes, and puggarees, and carrying white umbrellas, green and blue lined, were straying about among the flowers and under the heavy cypresses. Odours of roses and violets were wafted towards them from those last sleeping-places as they walked. Dark belts of shade were thrown from the sombre trees upon white marble crosses, birds sang loudly, unknowing of such things as death, and tears, and decay.

Two people—a tall man, and a girl dressed in grey—had wandered away a little from the rest of the group.

'Let us sit here, under the shadow of the great pyramid tomb,' said Oswald.

'How heavenly the calm and silence is!' he continued. 'We can't hear what the others are saying. Only the voices of the birds reach us, and what they talk of is much more in harmony with the peace and pathos of the place. Miss Routledge, do you know that you seem to me like an old friend already? I feel as if we must have met somehow, somewhere, before. It appears the most natural thing in the world that you and I should be sitting here alone together—for we *are* practically alone. I can ramble on to you as I have not been able to do to any one for a very long time; longer than I like to think.'

He looked at her sadly out of those wonderful dark eyes of his, and her foolish little heart gave a responsive throb under her grey dress.

'We mustn't stay here too long,' she answered nervously. 'And you—you remember that you told Mrs. Gadsden that you would yourself show her Keats's and Shelley's tombs. She is looking towards us now.'

'Yes, with those *fleur-de-tête* eyes fixed fiercely upon you,' said Mr. Oswald.

'I thought that you—that you rather admired Mrs. Gadsden?' said Miss Routledge quietly. 'You asked her for her photograph this morning when we were looking through Mr. Furber's groups.'

'Impossible! Did I? Well, it must have been in a momentary state of aberration. See, Miss Routledge, that lovely little lizard! Ah! there he goes—so quickly—past your shoe—into a fissure in that stone. Do you know the pretty legend of the lizard? Well, it is said that the Madonna—whose month it soon will be—the month of May—asked the serpent if he would be good to mankind? But he refused, and so he was told by her to crawl at the feet of the human race, with a curse for ever upon him. But the lizard, to whom she next turned, and asked the same question, said, "Yes—I will be good to the children of men." So Our Lady said, "Then you shall have legs to run on, and you shall be loved and cared for." And so he is.'

'That is pretty,' said Violet. 'I love all stories and legends about animals and birds. It seems to bring them nearer to us, to make us all more like one great family. Nothing can be more touching than the one telling us how it was that the robin got his red breast.'

'I don't know that one,' said Oswald, looking as if he thought the speaker much more interesting than any legend, but wishful to hear it so that he might prolong his *tête-à-tête* with her.

'Oh, you must have heard it! It is because he brought dew to poor souls in torment in the burning lake—and his feathers became red from being scorched by the flames. It is so pathetic an idea,' said Violet gently, 'that it seems to soften a little the grimness of the doctrine.'

Two or three figures came towards the pair —Mrs. Gadsden with lips turned down at the corners; Mr. Pepys, munching chocolate out of a paper bag; and Mr. MacClymont, the artist from Inverness. The latter was an admirer of

Miss Violet's, and not over pleased to see her engrossed by such a striking person as Oswald.

'I have brought out a sketching-block,' he said, in a slow, harsh voice, breathing mild reproof. 'If you would like to sit for an hour or so under that cypress, Miss Routledge, we could do a pretty bit of work together before we go home.'

Violet said that she did not feel inclined to draw or paint to-day, but that she would walk round the cemetery if Mr. MacClymont liked. Mrs. Gadsden gazed reproachfully at Mr. Oswald, 'You have not yet shown me poor Keats's and Shelley's graves,' she said. 'It's a great pity, though, that the inscriptions on them should be so heathenish, isn't it?'

Mr. Oswald shrugged his shoulders. 'I suppose theirs was the religion of most men,' he said coolly, but inwardly exasperated.

'You can't mean that,' cried Mrs. Gadsden, trying to be at the same time arch and reproving. 'You know you said at breakfast this morning, to Mr. Furber, that you always go to church yourself on saints' days—and that you had only given up fasting by the doctor's orders. *That* shows,' continued Mrs. Gadsden triumphantly, 'that *some* men have a great deal more religion than these poor deluded poets. Now, *are* you coming?'

Mr. Oswald stood watching the retreating

figures of Miss Routledge and the artist; and seeing that his pleasant *tête-à-tête* was doomed to cease, he turned graciously to the lady who lingered at his side.

'Of course I am. I particularly wished to stroll about with you, who are always so kind, and to look at these things that touch me more than I can say, in your sympathetic company. You remember Shelley's own description of this spot? He calls it the "most beautiful and solemn cemetery I ever beheld." Looking at the graves at his feet, he says of those buried here—"One might, if one were to die, desire the sleep they seem to sleep!" Curious, wasn't it, his saying that?'

'Most curious,' said Mrs. Gadsden, thinking as she spoke much of Mr. Oswald's beautiful voice, and but little of Shelley.

Another hour passed, and the party regretfully left the cool green slopes, the violet-scented air, and the shadow of the ivy-covered walls. Miss Routledge went upstairs to dress for the *table d'hôte* as if she were moving in a dream. She did not know when she had felt so buoyant—so full of strange hopes and tremulous joy, as she did to-night. As she came down the steps, loud noises of barking dogs—shrill ejaculations, oaths in the Italian and French languages, and a chorus of female shrieks, reached her ear. These all came through the entrance door. The reason was not far to seek. In the courtyard of the house two dogs were engaged in a ghastly tussle. The bigger of the two, a black mongrel, seemed in a fair way to demolish a beautiful little Roman dog, golden-haired, with a magnificent ruff and pointed nose. His owner, an old lady, who had dropped her card-case, her fan, and her handkerchief, was screaming, while the tears ran down her cheeks. Her footman, a voluble but helpless young man, wearing a brilliant cockade in his hat, was also yelling and waving foolish hands. The landlord gesticulated, the waiters ran aimlessly to and fro. Suddenly a tall Englishman rushed down the steps, through the excited groups, brandishing a stout stick in his hand. He ran towards the dogs, and promptly struck the black mongrel two heavy blows—one on his nose, and one on his forepaws. Then he wrenched him off his hapless little rival—how, no one seemed quite to know, but he did it. The small orange dog was bitten, but by no means fatally. And the valorous Englishman who had saved him appeared to the excited bystanders to be also bleeding. Anyhow he wound a handkerchief round his fingers, laughing as he did so. In a few seconds of time the mongrel was driven off, and the Roman dog clasped in his mistress's arms.

'O Monsieur, how can I thank you enough for your noble conduct! The act of a hero! Such self-devotion, such courage!'

The young man took off his hat and bowed gracefully. He was in evening dress, and some specks of blood disfigured his shirt-front.

'Great God! you are wounded!' cried the old lady. 'What can we do for you? Help! a basin—warm water—brandy, for this brave gentleman!'

Mr. Oswald only bowed again, and laughed. He really was hardly touched, he said. And it had been one of the greatest pleasures that he had ever experienced to save such a beautiful dog, and to gratify the distinguished lady whom he was now addressing. He spoke in fluent and graceful Italian.

'You will do me the kindness to call on me, sir,' said the old lady, touched as much by the extreme good looks of the dog's preserver as by the heroism of his behaviour. She handed him her card, on which was inscribed her name.

'The Princess ——'

Mr. Oswald bowed low again. He would assuredly do himself the honour to call on the Princess to-morrow. And, after a further interchange of pleasing civilities, the old lady and her dog were handed into her carriage. Mr. Oswald went up to change his shirt, and shortly afterwards returned to join the English party at dinner. His place was next to Mrs. Gadsden's. He smiled most kindly at her; but once, when she took up the bill of fare, he shot a quick, half-despairing glance across the table at Violet, who was sitting between the artist and the baronet who collected *curios*.

'You are going to-morrow to see the Princess?' said Mrs. Gadsden presently.

'Yes, she was nice enough to ask me.'

'*We* shall all seem very dull and flat to you if you take to going about in the best Roman society, I fear.'

'My dear Mrs. Gadsden, what can you mean? If I once make a friend, and I think I may say that I have made at least *one* here, no amount of fresh faces would put hers out of my mind. Ah! it might perhaps be better for me if it did.'

Yes, thought Mrs. Gadsden, as she looked first at her husband, now describing the Tiberine Museum to Mrs. Furber, then at Mr. Oswald —yes, there was no doubt about it, the latter *did* sigh. He was evidently not happy. How strange—he was so young, so gifted, so handsome! Perhaps she alone could help him, and prevail upon him to confide in her. Later on, when she came back into the *salon*, wearing a white burnous and new blue kid gloves, she walked straight up to him, a blush spreading over her sallow checks.

'My husband and I are going to a scientific

conversazione,' she said. 'Will you join us? I really think it may be pleasant.'

'Ah! why didn't you ask me sooner?' cried the young man in despairing accents. 'It is too tantalising and cruel of you! Just this *one* evening I have promised young Pepys to take him out to see a friend of mine, who expects us. I am terribly vexed.'

Poor Mrs. Gadsden's face fell. And when she went up to bed that night she noticed some odd blue marks on her face, which had been caused by an attempt to wipe away a few foolish stray tears with her gloved fingers.

CHAPTER III

Mr. Oswald was successful in inducing Mr. Furber to remain for a longer time in Rome than was originally mapped out in his carefully-arranged scheme. No one objected to spend another paltry thirty shillings or two pounds on such an unmixed pleasure. Perhaps the young man who had originated the idea was the means of adding a great part of the enjoyment to more than one of the travellers. Mr. Furber himself was impressed by his varied information, his linguistic skill, his even temper and boyish spirits. He was the most pleasant of companions whenever—and that was not now an unfrequent circumstance—he joined the English group and their clerical bear-leader. He often managed, so great was the urbanity of his manner, to soften the asperity of disobliging guides, and to make his way, followed by his troop of admirers, where the ordinary tourist was not allowed to enter. His friendship with the Princess ———, who had given him the run of her library and gardens, did not in any way seem to elate him, or to make him less cordial to humbler persons. He listened with deference to Mr. Gadsden's discourses, he took the greatest interest in Mrs. Furber's charities, and he had discovered different ways of amusing young Pepys, and of keeping him in a good temper. Mrs. Gadsden had of late become a little more out of spirits, and Miss Routledge less cheerful, otherwise most of the party were happy enough. Two events had nevertheless occurred which, but for the adroitness and ready tact of Mr. Oswald, might have served to place him on a less friendly footing with his compatriots. They had happened in this wise.

One evening Violet Routledge, accompanied by Miss Simpson and that lady's young brother, was strolling through the popular and beautiful gardens on the Pincian hill. The sublime view from the terraces was bathed in a purple haze, and hundreds of people were out enjoying the perfumed air, and the enchanting prospect at their feet. But Violet was feeling melancholy. She had hoped that Mr. Oswald would have joined them in their walk, and she had not seen him to talk to for a whole day and more, for Mrs. Gadsden had absorbed his attentions during the entire past evening. As she meditated, a hired carriage passed by close to her and her friends. Leaning lazily back in it, his hat a little on one side, a cigarette in his hand, and a laugh on his face that showed all his white teeth, she suddenly saw the object of her thoughts. Not alone. With some one evidently as amusing and lively as himself—a lady with the yellowest hair and the most scarlet lips that Violet had ever seen, dressed in the extreme of fashion, whose defiant eyes rested admiringly upon her companion.

Violet started, and her knees trembled.

As if by some intuition, Oswald turned his head sharply round, and changed colour ever so little. He hesitated for one second, and then took off his hat. The lady with the vermilion lips laughed.

'What a horrid-looking woman that is with Mr. Oswald!' exclaimed Miss Simpson. 'I'm sure she's painted up to her eyes. I can't admire his taste.'

Young Simpson laughed in a tiresome, enigmatical manner.

'I don't suppose that Oswald has the monopoly of it,' he said.

Violet walked on a little ahead, her heart sore and distressed. So it was for that vulgar creature that he had deserted her!

That evening at dinner she would not so much as look at Mr. Oswald. But in the evening he made his way to her side.

'Are you tired, Miss Routledge?' he said, 'or what is it? You are surely not quite yourself to-night?'

She turned her pretty head away.

'Have I vexed you, my dear little friend?' he said, very softly. Then she confronted him, looking straight into his eyes with her velvety brown ones.

'It's no compliment to me to be called a friend of yours!' she cried hotly.

Her meaning was clear to Mr. Oswald.

'Good gracious!' he exclaimed, 'you don't suppose that that silly little made-up Marchesa with whom I was driving is a *friend*? O dear no! She is not my sort, thank Heaven. Her husband is an old acquaintance of mine; but *he* is a delightful fellow, and she is not half good enough for him.'

'I am so sorry if I was cross,' said poor little Violet, happy and penitent. 'But Mr. Simpson said, you know, that——'

'Why attend to that gaping idiot? *Il vous*

en conte de belles! You surely might trust *me*, Vi—I beg your pardon, Miss Routledge.'

So she forgave him, and the matter was not again referred to between them. The other occasion upon which Mr. Oswald was nearly making an unfavourable impression occurred only a few days later on.

Mr. Furber had received a long letter from the Dean of —— containing many messages, and a small cheque for his dear son. Mr. Pepys had been dining out, and must have gone straight to his room on returning, the waiter said. So the clergyman mounted the stairs and hastened cheerfully to that young man's door.

'Who's there?' said a sulky voice from within, in answer to his knock.

'It's a letter, my dear Pepys—and a pleasant surprise for you from——'

Mr. Furber's spectacles and beaming red face looked through the open door. The surprise which *he* felt was probably greater than that which young Pepys would have enjoyed on receipt of his parent's cheque. Sitting at a small round table, with glasses at their elbow, and a half-emptied champagne bottle on a chair beside them, were two men playing cards. They were Mr. Galsworthy Pepys and Mr. Villiers Oswald. The latter rose, quite unembarrassed, with his usual bright smile.

'Well, my dear Mr. Furber,' said he, 'this looks desperately wicked and dissipated, and as if I were leading our young friend here into trouble. But the honest fact is that I have been suffering so awfully from sleeplessness, that I have asked Pepys to take a hand at piquet before I turn in, just to pass the time. I am more likely to get a good night if I sit up a little longer, you see. Moreover, it's only a "love" game, I needn't tell you that. And as to the champagne, I've been such a martyr to neuralgia since yesterday, that I thought I must have something to deaden the almost continuous and maddening pain.'

Mr. Furber no longer looked disconcerted. He was not by any means narrow-minded or prejudiced, but he was relieved to hear that the dean's son, at any rate, was not playing for money. He wished both men a cordial goodnight, and went creaking downstairs again in his heavy boots.

When the sound of his footsteps had died away, the younger of the players flung his cards and his cheque down on the table with fury.

'You're a cool hand, Oswald!' said he. 'Much use this beggarly cheque'll be to me now, when you've won twice as much from me already! I never heard any one lie as well as you do, however, I'll do you that justice.'

Mr. Oswald rose, with an uncomfortable

glittering expression in his eye that frightened poor Galsworthy Pepys, and would have surprised Mrs. Gadsden and Miss Routledge still more had they seen it.

'I may tell you, once for all, my young friend,' he said, in an icy, measured voice, 'that I do not tolerate that sort of observation from any one, least of all from a hopeless lout just home from school. I naturally thought it was to your advantage; it cannot matter a damn to me that that worthy old Furber should not think that you gambled. I shall now have the pleasure of returning to you the beggarly stakes that I have won; and of recommending you in the future not to play cards with men, but to join in a friendly round of "old maids" with Miss Hertz and Miss Simpson, or in a game of "beggar my neighbour" with Mrs. Furber.'

Mr. Oswald sat down again, took out a silver match-box, and lighted a cigarette.

'I'm not such a cad as not to pay when I've lost,' growled the boy.

Mr. Oswald smiled. The cold glitter had not quite died out of his eyes yet.

'Do you mind a cigarette?' he inquired courteously. 'Most of the other old women here kindly allow me to smoke in their presence, but if it distresses you——'

The boy banged his fist down upon the table.

'You know I'm no match for you in saying

nasty, cutting things,' he said with suppressed wrath.

'My dear boy, cheer up; don't look so glum! But I do not play with you again, remember that. And I am afraid I shall not be able to introduce you to the fascinating Mademoiselle Valerie, as I promised. For, no doubt, the dean and the minor clergy would object.'

Pepys got up, still scowling, and went to the window. He did not trust himself to speak.

Shortly afterwards Oswald tapped him gently on the shoulder. 'Now don't sulk,' he said. 'I only wanted to show you that I don't stand cheek. We'll find somewhere else to play if you like, and I will introduce you to the golden-haired siren to-morrow. But not a word about all this to any one. Surely, my dear Pepys, you must be sick of being treated like a baby? It's time you saw life for yourself.'

So the two made up their quarrel over the rest of the champagne.

CHAPTER IV

A DAY or two afterwards Mr. Furber had the pleasure of conveying his entire party on an excursion into the Campagna. Violet's spirits were again at high tide, for Mr. Oswald had of late devoted himself to her unceasingly. They had spent a delightful morning in the villa garden belonging to the old Princess, whose dog Villiers had rescued. They had wandered alone in the Colosseum by moonlight, and they had triumphantly escaped from Mr. Gadsden at the Baths of Caracalla, to enjoy a talk of the deepest interest as they sat together beneath a stretch of lichen-covered wall. But it must not be imagined that all these things had passed without comment and criticism. Poor Mrs. Gadsden went about with a dull pain at her heart, which surprised herself, and she had become disagreeably irritable. On the morning of the excursion to the Campagna, Miss Hertz and Miss Simpson were alone in the smaller reading-room of the hotel. The former began, in snappish tones—

'In spite, dear Miss Simpson, of that little Routledge girl's demure and cold manner' (Miss Hertz pronounced the last adjective 'code'), 'I, for one, would not trust her far. At Pisa, you remember, she got Sir Arthur Cracroft to dance attendance; and when he was laid up at Genoa, there was that spotty boy always running after her. Now, this time——'

'Yes, indeed!' said Miss Simpson grimly. 'Walking away by moonlight—with a gentleman, too, Miss Hertz! And, do you know, I have discovered that Mr. Oswald goes early to the markets, and brings her back flowers and fruit as well. Such apricots I saw in her room! I must say, though, she had the grace to offer me a few. Then there was a huge basket of plums, and one of little green almonds. It's really greedy and grasping, that's what I call it.'

'And flowers?' said Miss Hertz eagerly.

'I should *think* so! Roses and acacia-blossoms, and mimosa, and all sorts of yellow and purple wild-flowers.'

'She is a minx,' remarked Miss Hertz gravely. 'Oh!' with a change of tone, 'dear Mrs. Gadsden, you've got your hat on already! I must go and dress.'

Mrs. Gadsden came smiling into the room, followed by a tall, graceful figure, wearing a well-cut suit of light grey. He looked more provokingly handsome than ever as he bent over the clergyman's wife and said something which evidently pleased her.

'You can't really want it?' said poor Mrs. Gadsden, tremblingly drawing an envelope out of the pocket of her creased gingham skirt. 'It's my last copy, remember, and I'm afraid I look ever so much too young in it?' She ended her sentence in a half-wistful tone, hoping to be contradicted.

Mr. Oswald took the photograph in his hand and gazed earnestly at it. He had only yesterday remarked to Violet—

'Doesn't poor dear Mrs. Gadsden remind you of a boiled haddock? She has the sad and deprecating expression and the fulness of eye that we observe in that ever-popular fish.' So that it was curious that he should have desired to possess her portrait. But he had a keen sense of humour; and perhaps it amused him to see the pathetic earnestness with which she gave it to him. He put it carefully away in his pocket.

'I am dreadfully sorry that we have seen so little of one another lately,' said Mr. Oswald. 'How is it? You have always been talking to Sir Arthur or the Scotchman—or anybody, in fact, but me.'

At that moment Mrs. Gadsden really looked a pretty young woman. Her too prominent grey eyes shone with a soft light, and there was a brilliant flush upon her cheeks. She seemed about to say something, hesitated, and paused.

Mr. Oswald took her hand and pressed it to his lips. She started, and trembled from head to foot. So began and ended the first and last romance of the poor lady's monotonous life. It was doomed to be interrupted by the sound of steps and voices; and Mr. Furber, carrying his felt hat with its flowing puggaree, Sir Arthur, wearing a loose alpaca coat, which looked as if it had been bought off a peg in a second-hand shop, and MacClymont, with his sketching-block, appeared.

'We must make a start now, Mrs. Gadsden,' said Mr. Furber cheerfully.

Violet Routledge still looks back to those hours in the Campagna as belonging to one of the red-letter days of her not too bright existence. She shuts her aching eyes to pore over a mental picture of that great green panorama, with its background of mountains—rose and violet and sun-streaked. She sees the noble line of aqueducts touched with the golden fingers of the sinking sun—the quivering radiance lingering upon crumbling stones and trembling grasses. She watches the herds of patient dun-coloured cattle, marching slowly by, beautiful beasts with wide-spreading horns and velvet eyes. Here and there among them she remembers to have noticed a few of the melancholy and ugly buffaloes, ragged and short-legged, snorting as they walked with their heavy heads downbent. Then how lovely were the flocks of snowy sheep, with their picturesque shepherds in attendance—handsome, dark-eyed men and boys, with pointed hats and red waistcoats! There was one great white dog who allowed her to pat him as he walked alongside. What a day of delights it was! There were lovely goats, too, wandering among the ruins—animals with silky long hair;

and she recalls one—for no detail of that day is forgotten—who stood on top of a ruin and peered down through a chink at herself and her companion, with bright inquisitive eyes. As usual, she and that one other person had strayed away from the rest of the group. And he said—she can hear the musical echoes of his voice still—

'One feels as if one ought hardly to speak in prose here, in this divine place. Look at that corner of the aqueduct, shining like a fragment of a golden city. What a wonderful study of colour it all is! From the purple of the sky, growing deeper every moment, down to the masses of violet flowers at our feet.'

A group of peasants went by them a little way off. And they two stood still, watching the glories of sunset grow dim. Presently the stars came peering out, one by one. Everything was hushed into a tender silence. Then the sound of a bell, the Ave Maria, rang out in the perfumed air. A passing shepherd and his boy paused, their figures silhouetted against the peach-coloured sky, and reverently crossed themselves as they went homeward.

'Let us go back to the others,' said poor little Violet, feeling quite overcome by the beauty and romance of the scene.

'Must we go? Ah! yes, this perfect day is coming, or has come, to its end. I have some lines now ringing in my head as I look at you. Listen to them, dear—

> "And I know, while thus the quiet-coloured eve
>   Smiles to leave
> To their folding, all our many-tinkling fleece
>   In such peace,
> And the slopes and rills in undistinguished grey
>   Melt away——"

You know the poem?'

'I am afraid I don't,' said Violet, looking down at the long grasses and the purple flowers hardly visible in the dusk.

'Ah! this is how it goes on,' and his voice took a more emotional tone—

> "That a girl with eager eyes and yellow hair
>   Waits me there . . ."

'We *must* go back. Mr. Furber will be so angry with us,' and Violet took two faltering steps away from Villiers Oswald.

'No, stay, darling, hear the end.' He clasped her passive hand in his, a little hand that was very cold in spite of the warmth of this mellow evening.

> "When I do come, she will speak not, she will stand,
>   Either hand
> On my shoulder, give her eyes the first embrace
>   Of my face,
> Ere we rush, ere we extinguish sight and speech
>   Each on each."

That is something like a love-song!' said Mr.

Oswald, and he drew Violet towards him as he spoke. A change came over her.

'No, *no*!' she cried; 'I *must* go! We have been here too long already.' She wrenched her hand away and ran, rather than walked, towards the distant ruin where she had left the rest of the party. On arriving she was received with marked coldness by the ladies of the party. Even Mr. Furber, kind as he was, appeared a little distressed. Mrs. Gadsden's dreary, unsmiling face was bent upon her in gloomy disapproval. Miss Hertz and Miss Simpson spoke to each other in lowered and mysterious tones. But no one was vexed with Mr. Oswald. They only thought that Miss Routledge, the minx, pursued him. Back again in the hot, gas-lit *salon* of the hotel, poor little Violet found herself treated as a pariah. Mr. Oswald, too, purposely perhaps, avoided her, until as the ladies prepared to mount the stairs to bed he came up to her and said—

'Don't you think, now we know each other so well—I meant to ask you this before, but you ran away—that we might be less formal? Won't you call me "Villiers" when we are alone?'

Violet looked at him with her simple, direct gaze.

'I don't think Uncle John would like it,' she said.

Mr. Oswald smiled.

'What a conventional person you are, my dear little friend! But forgive me if I have vexed you.'

She wished him a hurried good-night, and sought the grateful loneliness of her own little room, perplexed, anxious, but happy somehow in spite of all.

CHAPTER V

'ONLY a week more! How sad it seems!'

The speaker was Miss Hertz, and she was partaking of long rolls and *café au lait* at breakfast in company with several friends.

'We shall have, at any rate, a most agreeable day for our excursion to Tivoli,' remarked Mr. Gadsden in precise tones. 'I purpose to give a short address at the tomb of Plautius Lucanus. We shall then walk leisurely towards the Villa of Hadrian, which, as you know, is now the property of the Government, with the exception of the south portion. Thank you, Mrs. Furber, a little more coffee, if you please. I will trouble you, Miss Hertz, for the hot milk. Nothing in Italy can compare, in my opinion, with these ruins. There were in former days an Hippodromus, lodgings for slaves, numerous temples, a serapeon of Canopus, and—thank you—I will take a little butter. Let me see— ah! yes. And there the Emperor was seized

with illness while residing in this glorious——
What's the matter?'

For Mr. Furber had joined the party, his face wearing a very lugubrious expression.

'I grieve to say,' he observed, 'that poor Oswald has received bad—extremely bad—news. His aunt—Lady Pitcairn——'

'Is dead?'

'No, but dangerously ill. He has to leave Rome this very day. It is too unfortunate, for he will miss Tivoli, and—and your delightful lecture, my dear Gadsden. We shall all feel quite lost without him, shall we not?'

'Yes, indeed,' said the ladies in chorus. And Mrs. Gadsden found that her roll and butter nearly choked her.

Mr. Furber cleared his throat.

'I had thought,' he said, 'that as this has been a singularly delightful and successful excursion to Rome, and as our kind young friend, Mr. Oswald, has to a great degree contributed to its success and pleasure, that it would be very—ahem! pleasant—hem! gratifying to us all, if we could give him some small token, some present, as a little souvenir—ahem! remembrance, of our very happy days together.'

Mrs. Gadsden blew her nose, and her husband spoke.

'A very graceful suggestion, my dear Furber. No doubt it is the idea, not the intrinsic cost of the offering, that will render it acceptable to our amiable friend?'

'I had thought of a *Church Service*, handsomely bound,' said Mr. Furber shyly. 'There is just time to get it and to present it before we start for Tivoli. It is only nine o'clock now.'

In an hour's time Mr. and Mrs. Furber re-entered the small reading-room adjoining the large *salon*, the former carrying a neatly done-up parcel. He was followed by all the ladies of the party and two or three of the men. Last of all came Mr. Oswald, already dressed for his journey, in a cool travelling suit, looking particularly serious, and with a tinge of melancholy in his beautiful eyes that was very becoming to him.

Good Mr. Furber was perfectly crimson. He wiped his forehead, coughed, removed his spectacles, and spoke—

'My dear friends—you will not expect—I am sure—a speech from me. I only wish—' and here he turned to Mr. Oswald—'to express in my name, and in those of my fellow-travellers, our warm gratitude to you for your indefatigable kindness in helping us all on—on many occasions. We desire—we hope—that you will accept this very—hem!—trifling memento of our—of our—may I say, friendship?—and we also trust that it may not be long before we have the pleasure of renewing an acquaintance that has been so—so—I may say—so delightful—to us all.'

Mr. Furber rubbed his handkerchief all over his face, came a step forward, and placed the parcel in Mr. Oswald's hands. The latter bowed.

'I am really too much touched,' he remarked, 'to do more than tender you all my deepest, warmest thanks. To me the memory of these weeks in Rome will ever have an inexhaustible and indescribable charm. I thank you all from my heart, and when——' here he raised his voice and looked—first at Miss Routledge, then at Mrs. Gadsden, lastly at the good clergyman —'*when* I use this book, I shall think with lasting gratitude of all the benefit and pleasure that I have received from you here.'

It was unfortunate that, owing to the projected excursion, Mr. Oswald should have to go alone to the station. But they saw the last of him as he stood on the doorstep watching his friends depart, giving a warm handshake to one, an affectionate greeting and smile to another.

Poor little Violet, whose heart ached unendurably, had determined nevertheless that she would not see him again alone. Some instinct told her, honourable and loyal as she was, that he had said too much, but yet not quite enough. 'If he really cares for me, he will write,' she said bravely to herself. So, although his eyes sought hers, and he tried to persuade her to come into the garden with him before she went to Tivoli, she shook her head. She began to wonder now if he had meant all or even a part of what he had said. She knew that she was not lovely, as he had insinuated, that she was only a nice-looking ordinary little girl, with a pair of very pretty eyes. But if he *had* spoken the truth, he would seek her and her uncle out in London, and then. . . . How idiotic it was of her heart to give such a wild leap when a wonderful possibility dawned upon her! Poor Mrs. Gadsden's face also appeared white and drawn as she stood upon the doorstep, and Oswald took her hand in his.

'I shall come and look you up in Lincolnshire,' he said, with a last sentimental gaze at her out of his flashing eyes.

'Oh! will you really? I think, somehow, you'll forget us all,' said she.

'My dear friend, could I ever forget *you*?'

And on this last sentence the poor lady meditated and lived during the whole of that long, hot, silent excursion to Tivoli, which, somehow or other, nobody much enjoyed.

It was very late when the party returned. The ladies went up, rather cross and silent, most of them, to their rooms to dress. Nearly all the English guests occupied rooms in a long passage on the second floor of the hotel. Miss

Routledge, and one or two more, lived on a higher landing. As the latter was putting the finishing touches to her simple gown, she heard voices, perturbed, angry, and excited, below her. Surely Mr. Furber's was one? She ran out and looked over the balustrade. Yes, there was the clergyman, scarlet, gesticulating, his hair unbrushed, and Mrs. Furber trembling and voluble beside him.

'It's gone, I tell you, it's gone!' cried Mr. Furber. 'Fetch Fritz—the landlord—everybody! My pedometer—the good one that Lord Conybeare gave me! And my—my box has been opened!' Here tears actually ran down Mr. Furber's face. 'The notes—all that I had put together for—for—for—the hotel bill —gone!' Mrs. Furber burst into tears.

'What carelessness! It's disgraceful!' she cried. 'O Signor Castello! it's all gone! Some one's been into Mr. Furber's room!'

Miss Hertz, wearing a dirty cashmere dressing-gown, rushed out of an adjoining door.

'My rigs, my rigs!' she screamed.

'O dear Miss Hertz, have *you* too lost something?' cried Mrs. Furber.

'All my jools, my ruby rigs, and my diamond rigs, and the brooches, and the——' Miss Hertz's stuffy voice became quite inaudible owing to her loud sobs.

Sir Arthur Cracroft, clad in a striped flannel

shirt, and wearing no coat, had joined the group. He appeared too angry to speak. At last, after many splutterings and incoherent noises, he made himself understood.

'My enamels—my watch set in pearls—my snuff-box with the miniature!' he shrieked. 'Where the devil are they? You've got thieves in this damned hotel!'

By this time there was a large concourse on the landing. Signor Castello, bowing, waving his arms despairingly; some dozen waiters, sympathetic, excited, or amused, came out and stared. Poor Miss Simpson was murmuring, 'I've lost my watch; I didn't take it to Tivoli. I wish I had.' But no one listened to her.

'Ah! *le farceur, le coquin!*' shrieked the old French lady, who had had nothing to lose, excepting a volume of sermons, which was still safe in her room.

Young Pepys came out of his room with a sort of grim mirth painted on his face.

'He's cleaned me out pretty well before,' he said.

'What do you mean?' screamed the ladies. 'He! Who? O Mr. Pepys, you surely don't, think——'

'*I* never thought him first chop,' pursued the young man doggedly. 'You were all desperately in love with him. I know how he laughed at you all!'

'It can't be—it *can't*!' and Mrs. Gadsden clutched hold of Mrs. Furber's arm. She seemed about to faint.

'We will inquire, we will search far and wide, my dear ladies,' said the landlord amiably, but vaguely. 'And, *en passant*, there is a large bill for wine left unpaid by the Signor Oswald. He has gone off, no one knows by what train, but he *has* gone.'

'O the villain! the brute!' cried Miss Hertz.

'He's one of your swell mob!' exclaimed the budding lawyer, Mr. Simpson. 'But we have as yet no proofs. Of course, taken together with the fact of his sudden departure, the probabilities are that he is a man of that stamp. But you can't at present prove it, and you won't see your things or the gentleman any more.'

'Pity you didn't scent all that out a little earlier in the day,' growled young Pepys.

No one noticed that Violet Routledge had gone back into her little room. She was absent that night from dinner, and on the following day was so ill with headache, and a touch of fever, that she did not come downstairs.

CHAPTER VI

THE Rev. Andrew Furber has taken other parties of tourists under his wing to Switzerland

and the Rhine and Sweden since the ill-fated excursion to Rome, of which he never talks very much. It is painful to him to think that he and his friends ever became intimate with such a depraved specimen of human nature as the gentleman to whom they presented the handsome *Church Service*. He no longer flatters himself on his powers of discernment. He has never recovered his pedometer, neither have Miss Hertz's precious stones been traced and restored to her, although some one, apparently very much like Mr. Oswald in personal appearance, has been taken up in Australia and convicted for forgery. Within her rifled jewel-case she found the following inscription scribbled upon an envelope: 'Who can find a virtuous woman? Her price is far above rubies. Although Miss Hertz's rubies are gone, her virtue is still left to her.'

But she has kept this added insult to herself; and Mr. Furber has never even confessed to his faithful wife that within his empty money-box was a scrap of paper bearing these words: 'Trust not in uncertain riches. The love of money is the root of all evil.'

Mrs. Gadsden has not joined Mr. Furber's parties again. She is thinner and sallower now than ever, and she becomes tired—inexpressibly tired sometimes—of the reiteration of school treats and mothers' meetings, and of the sight of the flat and marshy landscape of the Lincolnshire home where her lot is cast.

And poor little Miss Routledge, who has not much beauty left to her excepting her large, sad eyes, teaches music and drawing and history, and walks twice a day in Kensington Gardens, with no gleam of romance to gild her future, and only the most foolish of dead dreams to occupy her past. Sometimes when she sees a tall, dark man passing down a distant path, she starts a little. Can it be he? But it never is. Perhaps if it were, and if he came up to her once more with the old smile, and the voice that she sometimes thinks she still hears, she might even now forgive him, treacherous, unscrupulous, reckless as he was. But he is never likely to give her the chance. And, perhaps, all things considered, it is just as well.

A PAGE FROM A VICAR'S HISTORY

CHAPTER I

> 'Better ends may be in prospect,
> Deeper blisses (if you choose it);
> But this life's end, and this love-bliss,
> Have been lost here.'

HE stroked the head of his dog, and said good-humouredly to a child who stood by, 'Would you like to hear Oscar sing?'

'Oh, please!' cried the little girl, round-eyed with delight.

'Now, old boy, you've got to sing us a song!'

In a sweet tenor voice, bearing but little trace of age, the Reverend Charles Biddulph hummed a few bars of 'Auld Lang Syne.'

Curly black Oscar pricked up his ears, opened his wide jaws, caught the right note, and raised a plaintive howl, to the unbounded joy of the child.

'What a concert!' said another person at the front door. And a tall young man came through the house into the light which shone from the vicarage kitchen, towards the group there, blinking his eyes and laughing.

'Why, Algy! You are a late visitor!'

'I know. And I've come to supper with you instead of eating a solitary dinner at home, Let's have one of your excellent broiled bones, Mrs. Morris.'

The new visitor had a very pleasant and courteous manner. The cook smiled at him and curtsied.

'Thank you, my lord; I'll see what I can do.'

'Good night, Kitty,' said the clergyman to the child.

'Good night, sir; good night, your lordship.' She gave a little dip, and turned to leave the kitchen.

The young man who had just arrived laid his hand on the small girl's shoulder. 'Here's half a crown, Kitty, to buy a doll with.' Lord Kynoch was evidently in a very good temper.

'Now, Algy,' said the Vicar, as they went towards the front room, 'I suppose you have something to tell me.'

'How the dickens do you guess that?'

'My dear boy, from your manner. You are smiling all over your face. Yes—and actually blushing!'

The elder man threw his arm round the shoulders of the younger.

'I have suspected something for a little

while,' he said. 'Ever since you were at Monte Carlo, in fact.'

Lord Kynoch seated himself in an armchair in the study, under the rays of the Vicar's lamp. Seen in the bright light, he was less prepossessing than he had appeared in the hall. His complexion was unhealthy, with a certain redness round his eyes and nose; his fair hair was thin and lustreless; his hand shook a good deal as he adjusted the lamp-shade, which his elbow had displaced. The Vicar looked at him for one moment sharply out of his dark eyes. Then he sighed.

'You are not looking very well to-night, Algy.'

The young man moved restlessly in his chair.

'Oh, it's nothing. I'm rather jumpy, that's all. I sat up so late all last week.'

'I thought so.'

'And of course I'm excited about what I've to tell you. You see'—and the young man rose and took the Vicar's firm hand in his own trembling one—'you're my very best and truest friend, and I don't know how you'll take it.'

'I want you to be very happy, Algy.'

'Well, so I am. I know—although, of course, you're in favour of a celibate clergy and all that—you want a man like *me* to marry. And that's what I'm about to do!'

'I am rejoiced,' said the Vicar. 'Who is she, Algy?'

'Well, that's just it, you know.' Kynoch's hand shook more than ever. 'My relations—and it's just like their d——d interference—I beg your pardon; I mean they don't seem to take any interest in me except when they want to annoy. *They* don't approve at all.'

The Vicar looked inquiringly at his friend.

'You're not a Pharisee; *you're* not narrow,' blurted out the young man. 'So I'll tell you there *were* some stories about her years ago, and she's older than me—a good bit. She's always lived abroad, so really it's nobody's business here but mine.'

'I don't know that it is; but I did want you, Algy, to marry some one who—well—I'm not going to preach. You know your temptation, and you've been giving way again, I see. I wanted you to marry some one who'd help you.'

'So she will, because I care for her so desperately.'

And poor Kynoch's face became almost transfigured. 'She's beautiful and clever, and she likes me. And if that's not enough, I'd like to know what, in God's name, is?' His voice shook painfully.

'Have you known her long?'

'Not so very. Only abroad. She's not been in London for years and years. What does it matter whether she's forty or not, if she looks young? I don't care a hang!'

He hit the table violently with his clenched fist.

'Come in to supper,' said the Vicar gently. 'You shall tell me more presently.'

The two men seated themselves at a small round table. Kynoch looked rather forlornly round the room.

'I say, couldn't you let me have a whisky-and-soda?'

'I'm afraid you must put up with my light claret this evening. And now, what is the lady's name? You are a sort of son to me, Algy, you know; ever since I gave you lessons all those years ago, when you were a funny little chap in a kilt; and so she must be a daughter.'

'Thank you; upon my soul, you *are* a good friend. Her name is Madame De Morel. She's a widow.'

'And when will the wedding be?'

'Well—she's not sure about that—I suppose because she thinks my relations don't want her. She won't exactly promise me, you know. But she is sure to—I hope quite soon. She's coming here, with a connection of hers as chaperon, on a visit next week.'

At eleven o'clock Lord Kynoch walked home through the broad park towards his house.

Arrived there, he unlocked a case of bottles, drank half a tumbler of whisky, and went to sleep, still dressed, in a large armchair.

CHAPTER II

ABOUT a week after Kynoch's visit, the Vicar was returning from the house of a parishioner, now lying seriously ill in a distant farmstead. Although frosty, the air was so still that Mr. Biddulph did not quicken his pace as the evening drew on.

A round scarlet November sun peered at him with a face that seemed half-friendly, half-mocking. The undulating fields, and a shining stream visible here and there as it crossed them, were dashed with crimson. The red glare caught, too, an edge of the pyramidal spire of the small church, of Norman date, standing some two hundred yards away. One solitary and giant yew waved protecting arms round the massive tower, rising but little above the roof. Ivy grew luxuriantly over the deep-recessed doorway. The evening light became momentarily rosier and more glowing, glorifying the grey stones and the curves of the outspreading boughs. Mr. Biddulph watched the sunset, as he had often done for some twenty springs and autumns—from this same tranquil spot; when the roses were blooming

over the silent graves, and when the icicles
hung upon the mouldings of the windows, and
the birds left forlorn and tiny footprints on the
snow-covered roof. Oscar came and leant his
head against his master's knee. Lost in
thought the Vicar stood, the panorama in
front of his eyes growing sublimer as he gazed.
Low upon the horizon was a deep flaming gulf,
which might have been the waters turned into
blood by the prophet of old. Higher spread a
sea of tenderest blue, shading into primrose,
with a boundary of swarthy clouds that to the
Vicar's poetical fancy seemed a belt of perilous
cliffs. And right in the middle of the melting
yellow ocean shone one tiny star, in a solitary
beacon seeming to light the clouds now moving
as ships across the trackless expanse. The red
glow illumined Mr. Biddulph's fine head and
thoughtful eyes. It was the face of a man who
had suffered and struggled, and found something of peace, if not exactly joy; a type
oftener seen perhaps in an Italian ascetic than
in an Anglican clergyman. Closely cropped
iron-grey hair, and cheeks very much sunken,
lent character to the sensitive, delicately cut
lips and dark eyes deeply set.

Just below the hill from which he was gazing
was a hawthorn-tree, with bare brown twigs
drooping beneath the weight of a myriad
crimson berries, and shining in the evening

light like clusters of coral. This beautiful tree had evidently also attracted the admiration of a lady in the road below the slope of the hill, for she, too, stood still, looking up at the branches, the sunset lustre turning her fair hair to dazzling gold. She was a tall woman, richly dressed, with a quantity of soft grey fur round her neck, and wearing a hat adorned with the same trimming.

'Ah!' thought the Vicar. 'That must be Madame de Morel. Algy said she was to arrive yesterday.' He observed that she was graceful and slender as a girl, though possibly she might have been over forty. 'I will go and introduce myself to her, as I am a sort of father and guardian to her future husband. Yes, I certainly think I may.'

He strode quickly forward. The lady heard his step ringing on the frosty road, and turned her head.

The Vicar stopped suddenly and breathed hard, moved a foot's pace onward, and paused again, as if enfeebled.

The lady grew very white beneath two patches of unchangeable red on either cheek. But she walked straight towards the Vicar, her hands outstretched.

'Oh, my God! Charles!'

And he said, drawing near, and taking the hands in his own, which had suddenly grown icily cold—

'Is it you—*really* you?'

. . . .

Mr. Biddulph and Madame de Morel did not return straight to the village. Near the tree with its load of berries a side lane branched off—a solitary way where deep ruts were frozen into hard little banks round the ice patches. The red was dying away in the western sky; the church now looked a mere dark silhouette in the midst of a dun landscape.

The woman was the first to speak.

'I wondered what had become of you—whether you were dead or——'

'I only wish to God I were!'

The lines round the Vicar's face had become profound furrows, and his mouth was contorted into an expression of pain and unrest strangely foreign to his face and to his usually devotional repose.

'Let me try to collect my thoughts a little, Adelaide,' he continued, in a broken hoarse voice. 'After—after you went away—ah! do you remember the anniversary was last week?—I stayed and worked on in London as well as I could. It chanced that one Sunday a lady was in my church who had had a very sad and suffering life. Something I said in my sermon came home to her. She asked to see me in the vestry, and confided in me. She had been married to a brutal and drunken husband, and there were other troubles. She told me that she was now alone with her little boy, and that the living at her place was vacant. She made but little doubt that I could have it, if I would take it, for she knew something about the work we had organised in London. I was sick at heart in the old place—in the house where you and I had been together, Adelaide—worn out, disheartened, ill. Briefly, I came away, here, to this quiet village. Lady Kynoch always remained a very true and good friend to me, and she never inquired into the details of my past. I taught her boy Algy, and soon began to love him as my own child. Poor fellow! he has made a sad disaster of his life in some ways, but I cannot think him altogether responsible. Much of his temptation—you know what this is!—is doubtless an inherited one. He has such good impulses, and in spite of his failings he is a true gentleman at heart. What—what'—and the Vicar turned his dark eyes upon his companion—'is to become of him, as well as of you and me? I haven't been able yet to grasp all that this meeting means—the present agony of it, the future misery and despair of it.'

He lowered his voice, and his face was bent upon the ground.

Madame de Morel gazed furtively at him, at the noble outlines of his profile, the tortured expression in his mouth. They had reached the end of the lane, where a path branched across the fields towards the Hall.

'What can *I* do?' she said in imploring and forlorn accents. 'You know I began this innocently. It seemed a relaxation, a relief, Charles. Of course, I did not mean to let it go far. I dare say you won't believe me?'

A vision of poor Kynoch's transfigured face as he had told the Vicar of his love flashed across the latter's mind.

She continued—'I suppose you—you knew, you heard, and guessed something of what my life has been—what it gradually became after I left you? But you don't know all the wretchedness and iniquity of it. I couldn't tell you—a clergyman, a man whose life is spent in prayer and meditation and doing good. I grew to care only for money and luxury and the lowest side of things. I went all over the world—no, don't wince; I am not going to say much more to hurt you. Then my fate brought me to Monte Carlo. I met Lord Kynoch, and he liked me in a different way, somehow, from the others. He believed in me. He seemed to see me as I was when I was a girl, before I began that cursed existence away from you. He offered me real affection. I did feel sometimes that I had no right to accept it; but then, again, I knew that he had been wild, that he still drank, and I thought I could be of more use to him than a woman who had seen less of the rough side of life. So I could not bring myself to dismiss him. For the same reason, when he proposed to me, I could not say no all at once; and, having passed as a widow, it was difficult to explain to him that you were probably living. So I allowed things to drift on. You know the rest. And now—and now——'

Large tears gathered in her eyes, and fell upon the grey fur round her neck.

'I don't reproach you,' said the Vicar slowly.

'I couldn't—I *couldn't* ask you to take me back!' she moaned. Her tears began to choke her. 'Me—*me* in a country vicarage! Me, the wife of a clergyman like you! It is an impossibility, even if *you* wished it.'

He lifted his eyes, shining with unshed tears. He was thinking of her as she had looked twenty years ago, when her head had rested on his shoulder, and her arms had been flung around his neck. Now the night and the day, the dawn and the twilight, the stars and the dim lights twinkling in the distant village, were not farther apart than they two.

At last he took her shaking hand in his. 'Adelaide, my poor little girl.' It was the old kind voice that she had not heard since she was young, when he had loved her so blindly. 'I don't want you to go away fancying that I have one hard thought of you. Those have all gone long ago. Every day I have prayed for you, my wife, as I used to do when we were together, and you cared just a little for me. Whether you were living or dead I thought my prayers might still, perhaps, not be all useless; but I don't think that I ever hoped or wished to see you face to face *here*—not till '—his voice sank to a whisper—'our hearts have been purified by this suffering and our bodies gathered to the dust. If you came under my roof, it could not be as a wife. And the story of your past would be whispered about and be ever dogging you and haunting you. I must say good-bye to you, little girl—till the old things have passed away and we begin a new existence elsewhere—one quite unlike this!' He had dropped, unconsciously, into his former way of speaking to her—the gentle, caressing accents that sounded like curious echoes of a dead past.

'Good-bye!' she said, her lips quivering. Then she added: 'And Algy?'

'*He* must not know. It is cruel for him. Poor Algy!'

'I will say I have thought over his proposal of marriage again and the unwisdom of it—or, better still, I will go when he is out shooting to-morrow, and write to him from London.'

The Vicar groaned. It was torture to him to think of Kynoch's pain.

'And it seemed the beginning of so much better days for him,' he said below his breath.

The earth was lying in shadow now. The distant church clock struck, and more lights appeared over the fields in the Hall windows. Silently the pair retraced their steps down the road, which was growing every moment harder and stiffer in the frost. Adelaide shrank from crossing the dusky pastures alone, and the Vicar felt that they could not be seen together with such traces of emotion in their faces. They reached the high-road again. Once more he took her hand.

'God help you, poor little girl!' he said.

And she looked the while so unlike a girl, so old and haggard, standing in a patch of wan light from one disconsolate oil-lamp, that seemed rather to increase than illuminate the gloom around them.

'You have been very good to me, Charles,' she whispered. They were quite alone in the still, cold country road. Two or three labourers were walking away from them a long way in advance.

'Will you kiss me just once?' she said, and then shrank away from him as if terrified.

He bent down and touched her forehead with his lips, and she felt his tears falling on her face as he gave her that one last kiss.

CHAPTER III

'Is the Vicar at home?'

The question was asked in a strained, broken voice, and the questioner, hardly waiting for a reply, forced his way past the servant into the study.

The clergyman rose from his writing-table, turned round, and confronted Kynoch. The faces of both were pale and haggard, as if neither of them had slept. There were red rims round Algy's eyes, and his mouth twitched convulsively. It was evident from his aspect that he was not entirely sober, and he seemed to find a great difficulty in forming his words. The result was that he uttered them at last very loudly and slowly, and in husky tones.

'She has gone away! . . . without a word of good-bye, leaving me just this!'

The young man put a note into the Vicar's hand. Then, without warning, he sat down and broke into passionate weeping, terrible to see.

'What—what the devil—I ask you—does she mean? We were going to be so—so happy! I know I had a little too much of that champagne—infernal strong stuff it is—last night. But she's seen me like that before. She writes, you see—why, in God's name, don't you *read* it, instead of staring at me? I don't want your pity, I tell you! I'm for action—I must take a strong line, do something, go for her—bring her back—fetch her . . .'

The pitiable contrast between his violent words and his weak, shaken frame struck the Vicar painfully. But the latter scarcely knew as yet how to answer him. And poor Kynoch went on raving the while and shedding tears, swearing, walking round and round the little room, appealing, imploring.

Mr. Biddulph tried to quiet him.

'We will think it over, Algy.'

'What the devil is the use of your thinking? Little interest people like you seem to take when things don't affect themselves!'

Mr. Biddulph had become ashy white.

'I'll tell you what,' said Kynoch, sinking into a large chair and changing his tone. 'You *can* do something for me! You're accustomed to preach and give advice. You shall go to London and see her, and tell her she must come back! I'm going to reform, I won't take a single glass of spirits. Upon my soul I won't, if she comes back, I swear it to you!' He laid his hand imploringly upon the Vicar's shoulder. 'You'll do this? you'll help me?'

Mr. Biddulph trembled.

'I am afraid—I very much fear—I cannot take steps——'

Then Kynoch broke out into a torrent of

violent and profane words, for which, to do him justice, he was but partially responsible just then. He shook the Vicar by the shoulder, clenched his fist, then turned suddenly, banged the door, and strode away out of the house.

That same evening, like another transgressor of old, he, too, poor fellow, came to himself again, and then he retraced his steps towards the Vicarage. Mr. Biddulph was out, the maid said. 'He has gone to see a woman who is dying, right over there.' And she vaguely pointed towards the chalky outline of the distant downs. Poor Kynoch was bitterly disappointed; he was by this time heartily ashamed of himself, and he thereupon sat down in the clergyman's study and wrote him a note, in very shaky characters:—

'MY DEAR VICAR,—I spoke to you like a blackguard this afternoon. Can you ever forgive me? You have been so good to me all through my wretched life, a life which has disappointed you and everybody else who had any hopes for me. It's too late now to amend, I fear, but I want you to believe I am more sorry than I can ever tell you in words for my rudeness. I behaved like an absolute cad. As to the other matter—I am simply heart-broken. I will come again to-morrow evening and ask your advice once more.—Ever yours,

'ALGY.'

The following afternoon, Mr. Biddulph, who had forgiven his former pupil long before he found and read his letter, was preparing to walk up to the Hall, when a groom with a horror-stricken face appeared at the door.

'What is it?' said the Vicar anxiously.

'Bad news, sir. His Lordship was driving that there new mare of his with the nasty temper towards Crofton Hill. She took fright near the level crossing and smashed up the trap, sir; and Thomas, he's knocked silly, and his Lordship...'

The Vicar felt his heart stand still.

'They've carried his Lordship up to the Hall, sir. That's why I've come. He do look awful bad, they tell me.'

'Is he insensible?' Mr. Biddulph spoke in a curiously calm voice, like a man who talks in his sleep.

'Oh yes, sir! They've sent for Dr. Barnes, and I expect he's there by now. I've got a dogcart, sir, if you'll come along with me at once.'

When the Vicar's eye fell upon the bruised face and battered form of his young friend he knew that there could be little or no doubt of the issue of this day's misfortune. If Lord Kynoch had lived on, said the doctor, there would be paralysis of the lower extremities. But the other injuries were so severe that it was a mercy to think, perhaps, that such a fate could not be his. For a slow dragging space the Vicar watched by the dying man, patient as a father, tender as a woman who mourns by her child's bedside. Two or three hours or so before the end came Algy spoke to him.

'I've got one wish, Vicar.'

'Yes, my boy?'

'I want to see *her*, if I could, just to tell her I forgive, and understand. She was quite right to give up such a brute as me!'

'Hush, hush! don't talk. It will hurt you so, my dear.'

'Can you send for her?'

The Vicar trembled a little. 'I could—if you wished it very much,' he said, after a moment's pause.

'Telegraph,' whispered Algy.

And a message was flashed to London. In about forty minutes' time the answer to it came—not from Madame de Morel—from a doctor in London. It ran thus:—

'Grieved to say was called in to attend Madame de Morel this morning. She was suffering from severe headache last night, and took chloroform upstairs with her. Unfortunately, stopper came out of bottle. She was found insensible, and I discovered life to be already extinct.'

The Vicar felt a sudden faintness seize him.

There was brandy by Kynoch's bedside. Half unconsciously, he drank some of it. For one moment, in his new and desperate agony, he half wished that the sick man's eyes would never open again to inquire the result of the message. He buried his haggard face in his hands, and, after a few seconds of torturing conflict, lifted it. Then it bore a changed expression, sweet and spiritual. He was much calmer now. God knew best, after all, he thought. That truth seemed to him surer than ever before.

Then Algy looked up at him.

'Will she come?'

'Yes; she will.' The clergyman spoke with conviction. 'Shut your eyes, dear, and try to sleep till then.'

The Vicar went across the room to the writing-table, and wrote another message. So the weary agonising minutes dragged on. Algy moved his head restlessly. The clergyman came up to the bedside.

'She may be too late,' said Kynoch. 'But if it's true what you say about heaven, and all that—will she—will she—belong to me there perhaps, as I'm so sorry? . . .'

A spasm of pain passed over Charles Biddulph's face, and a feeling of revolt through his heart. Could he bear to give her up, even in some other new state of life? Was she not his own wife still, whom, God help him, he loved, and had loved, and still must and would love through all the eternities? He knelt down by the bedside.

'Algy, can you attend if I say one short prayer?'

'I only want *her*,' said the dying man. 'Tell me, *is* it true that she and I will be together in heaven? If I thought that, perhaps I might pray.'

The Vicar bowed his head.

'You will see her, I believe, Algy, in a state of existence where there will be no more misunderstandings, no cruel farewells, my dear, no pain.'

Kynoch became very quiet. Once Mr. Biddulph saw his lips move. He stooped to catch the words. They seemed to him to sound like ' Together . . . no pain . . .'

CHAPTER IV

THERE were people who wondered at the self-control and calm bearing of the Vicar of Sedgebrook when he read the funeral service to a crowded congregation standing solemnly by the great yew-trees. Women sobbed, the men brushed their eyes with their coat-sleeves as two coffins were lowered side by side into the dark vault where so many of the bones of poor

Kynoch's ancestors already lay. On one brass plate was inscribed the name—

'Algernon, eighth Viscount Kynoch.'

On the other, 'Adelaide de Morel.'

So she had come back to him again.

As the last group left the churchyard the agent's wife said to her husband—

'John, all this has made me feel quite ill. To think of those two who were to have been married, and so happy! How could Mr. Biddulph possibly be able to stand up and read without crying?'

'People sometimes feel most who don't cry.'

'True, and he does look awfully thin in the face. I don't fancy either, John, that his hair was so white when we saw him a week ago.'

'I don't think it was.'

Then the pair turned homewards. And meanwhile a solitary man dressed in black, his hand resting on his dog's head, stood at the Vicarage window, looking blankly out at the now deserted graveyard.

'So this is the end, Oscar!' he said.

. . . . . .

When the spring came, other and new faces and figures flitted through the Hall corridors, over the green tennis-lawns, and down the village street. Algy Kynoch was fast becoming only a memory to everybody but one lonely old friend. Men in London said—

'Yes, poor chap—nobody could go on at that rate. I've seen him drink six or seven whiskies-and-sodas in an afternoon.'

And others echoed: 'Yes, he was a perfect wreck! Odd story about the Frenchwoman, too, whom he was to have married. It really was a mercy, perhaps, that he didn't live to make such a fool of himself. She would have kept poor old Algy alive though, if it's true what one heard of her!'

Mr. Biddulph and Oscar, who was growing very old and feeble in his movements, lived on quite alone together, as before. The new people at the Hall, Algy's cousins, voted the Vicar's sermons and conversation dull.

'And he's really rather a depressing person, dear,' said one of the girls to a friend. 'I suppose he thinks us all too noisy, and our jokes vulgar, for he hardly spoke twice when he came to dine last night. *I* don't believe—though, of course, he does his duty by the poor, and they're very fond of him, I hear—that he cares for any company but his own and that of his old dog.'

Perhaps this last remark had a good deal of truth in it. When a man has given all his love and most of his thoughts to just two people for twenty years and more, and these objects are suddenly snatched away by some deadly blow, as bitter as unforeseen, it is unlikely that he will form new ties, especially if he happens to have already passed five decades of life.

The Vicar works on still and waits. And no one guesses the while how much of his heart is buried with the two who lie side by side under the shadow of the great yew-trees that he sees so plainly from his windows. A weak and dissolute man, a sinful, passionate woman, resting so near him and yet so far, in a last dreamless sleep.

AT THE SIGN OF THE STARTLED FAWN

> 'The meadows are waving high,
> With plumy grasses of grey,
> And gold-eyed daisies are born;
> There's a lark in the silvery sky,
> And a thrush on the wild rose spray,
> And poppies in the green corn.'

THE old inn stands back some thirty yards from the broad white road, from which the hot dust flies to-day in blinding clouds. A chestnut-tree on one side gives an oblong patch of shade that overspreads a long deal table flanked by two benches. A weeping willow faces the chestnut, and under its no less grateful shadow is a smaller table of iron, and also a chair or two. Beneath the projecting gables of the inn some one has hung baskets of differing sizes, all ablaze just now with a bewildering mass of geraniums, pink, and scarlet, and darkest crimson. These trail in graceful garlands over the window cornices, and from below no less dazzling festoons of roses, deep red and apricot-coloured, climb up to meet them.

Although the house lies in shadow, it has an illuminating glow all its own, emanating from these flowers. As I stopped at the door, one afternoon last June, a man led out a white horse, and watered him at a trough by the weeping willow. He went slowly away, singing a verse of the last music-hall stave, while the landlady's blackbird hanging hard by looked out through his wicker bars, and chattered in the peculiar agitated note of his race as a cat stalked along the window ledge. It was only for the sake of attracting attention; he knew that the tabby would not risk a single one of his lives by touching a feather of Mrs. Dunlop's pet.

A little breeze came soughing through the chestnut leaves, and moved the faded signboard ever so gently. The hinge creaked, and the startled fawn, whose painted coat is very dingy at the present day, quivered on his wooden panel as if he were going to bound away into the dusky thicket by which he stands. A farmer pulled up his cart in front of the door, helped his goodwife to clamber out, and called for the barmaid. Then a man on foot joined them, and the three ordered beer for the farmer and ginger-ale for the lady, and sat peacefully down within the cool shelter of the glossy leaves. It was an ideal June day, one that I could have wished to be prolonged into infinity;

the sky all transparent blue, with only a single cloud like a small white hand floating over my head. When I descended at the inn door I had already driven some eight miles along the hard white road, and feeling hot and thirsty, I asked for some wine and soda-water, and sat down on the bench.

Throughout my drive my senses had been revelling in the panorama of colours, the bird-life in the fields, the air heavily sweet with the odours of honeysuckle and hay and elder-blooms. The roadside banks were brilliant with the lilac of the tall mallows. Among the waving green of the corn-sheaths there were wide patches of blood-red, where the poppies grew in their thousands, and the blue cornflowers, now in full beauty, nodded their heads beside them in glowing profusion. It was a scene of brilliancy without gaudiness—flashes of colour and light that passed me by, and left no impression of over-garishness upon the brain.

Mr. Dunlop, the landlord, remarked that we were having quite the finest June that he had seen for some fifteen years past.

'And what a splendid Ascot it was too, sir! I and my good lady, we went as usual on the Cup Day, and we had a grand view this time. His lordship, sir, he looked quite pale when he led his horse in. The people did cheer him too. He's very popular, is Lord Eddington in these parts. Always a nice civil word for every one, and her ladyship the same.'

Mrs. Dunlop had joined her husband and myself, and was blinking beneath her hand at the white road.

'There he comes!' said she, 'and my lady too, in his phaeton.'

A dust-cloud swirled round the chestnut tree, powdered the scarlet geraniums, and made Mr. Dunlop cough noisily.

'It's a funny world,' he said presently, when his choking fit was over. Then he solemnly continued—

'Times is changed—some says for the better, some says for the worse. I've no reason to be down in the mouth, because our business always pays pretty well alike. Has it struck you, sir, that one don't hear of quite so many scandalous things in these parts as used to go on? Not but what'—here Mr. Dunlop folded his arms over his redundant figure—'some of the nobs are shady enough still. But in this particular place they've taken a turn for the better. So it strikes me.'

'Indeed, yes, at Eddington especially, that they have,' said Mrs. Dunlop, still straining her admiring eyes after the dust-cloud. 'Do you mind it, John—it was just this week as ever is, the week after Ascot races, twenty years since, when we had that unpleasantness here in this house with the late lord?'

I could hardly forbear smiling at this phrase of the good woman's, for I knew something, though but vaguely, of the tragedy which her words recalled.

'I'm in no hurry, Mrs. Dunlop,' I said. 'I am going back to London by quite a late train. Why not tell me the story? I've heard, of course, just a little about it, but it would be interesting to have all the details from one who was on the spot.'

'Dear, dear!' and Mrs. Dunlop gave a fat sigh of retrospection. 'It was a bad job. I always say to everybody I know, Marry, I say, in your own spear, whatever it may be, 'igh or low, if you wish for 'appiness. But I like young Tom Drax, too. He was a fine young man— and on his way to the races he'll often stop now and have a chat. A perfect gentleman he is, no doubt of that!'

'Well, Mrs. D., just you get on with this story of yours—or late train, or early train, the gen'leman won't hear much of it!' said Mr. Dunlop, preparing to light up his pipe.

I drew up an armchair close to the table, and invited Mrs. Dunlop to take another beside me. Her husband yawned, stretched himself, and went lumbering off to talk to a local horse-dealer, whose smart trap cast a shadow across the doorstep. Then the landlady told me all about some events that had happened at the

'Startled Fawn' twenty years ago. I will give the substance of her narrative in my own less graphic words, as hers were occasionally breathless and incoherent, and I could not possibly remember either the number or the diversity of the ejaculations with which the story was adorned.

. . . . . .

It was the week after the Ascot of 187—, and a day of warmth, sunlight, and colour. A group of more or less heated men were sitting outside the inn porch discussing the past races, the coming harvest, and the doings of the neighbourhood in general. The social qualities and conduct of the greatest land-proprietor in the district, Lord Eddington, were freely commented upon, and in a strain that was hardly flattering.

'No one'd take 'im for a gen'leman,' said a thin man in black, who followed the profession of tax-collector. 'His languidge, they all tell yer, would lift the tiles quite off yer roof. And what with his short neck, and that vulgar face of his under his white hat that makes it look ever so much redder—why, any one'd be astonished to see 'im take a fust-class ticket to go racing.'

'Of course, to give the devil his due, he didn't have much of a time of it when he was a little chap,' said Mr. Fuggle, who had supplied Eddington Hall with lamp-oil ever since the present owner was an infant, and could therefore speak with authority. 'The old lord couldn't, usually speaking, walk steady after five o'clock, and it's a fact he never got out of bed till just upon two. As to her ladyship, dook's daughter or no dook, we all know the kind of games she was up to. Eh! she was a warm lot!'

'Right enough,' said Mr. Dunlop, 'and I've no doubt that the present lady, though she's merely Old Brunner's daughter, is a pounds better bred 'un than a lord like this husband of hers. Still, as my good woman often says to me,—"you should marry in your own spear!" And if old Brunner's an honest chap, he's still a bookmaker, though he may take a villa on the river—and go puffing up and down it in his swell steam launch.'

'He's a highly respectable man, is Brunner.' Mr. Fuggle spoke with conviction. 'You may or may not 'old with his calling, that's a matter of taste, I say, but you can't deny he's a good sort for what he is.'

'Far be it from me to deny it,' remarked Mr. Gamble, a fat farmer, pompously. 'As for callings, Mr. Dunlop, Mr. Brunner lent his dining-room for the Sunday-school when the measles was in the real building. And those two girls of his, Lady Eddington and her sister, were always as quiet and nice as you'd wish to see. They don't go about on the river hollering to young men, and sprawling about in punts, like some of your smart ladies. I'm uncommon sorry for that poor soul, Lady Eddington. I saw her at Ascot, when that precious husband of hers was in one of his towering rages. He'd have killed the horse, or the boy who was up, and didn't win, or his wife and anybody else handy, if he could have done it.'

'I saw him too,' said another farmer. 'His face was red as a raw beefsteak. And there he was swearing quite disgusting at that poor wife of his. Before everybody, too, calling her such terrible names. She went quite white when she clambered up on the box-seat beside him. Well, all I can say is, I wouldn't like Mrs. Dunlop here to know the shameful things he called that poor creature.'

The landlady had drawn close to the group, and was listening with interest. 'I've never seen Lady Eddington,' said she, 'but she was a foolish girl to marry as she did, I shall always say. I knew her poor mother when she was employed at the bar at the "Wheatsheaf." A nice quiet young person. Mr. Brunner was a great catch for her, of course.'

'Ah! Miss Edith Brunner never did a sillier thing than when she went to church with that foul-mouthed young brute, lord or no lord,' said Mr. Gamble. 'Young Tom Drax is wild after her still, I'm told, and the Draxes, father and son, is, as you know, in the same line of business, Mrs. Dunlop, as old Brunner, so it would have been quite suitable. There ain't a racecourse where you don't see Tom. He's a head and shoulders taller than most chaps, and a fine-looking feller all round.'

The barmaid came out of the porch and whispered to the landlady—

'There's a young woman at the back door asking for you, ma'am.'

'All right, all right,' said Mrs. Dunlop, a little vexed at being interrupted. 'What does she want?'

'She looks awful ill, ma'am. So I asked her to take a seat in the back kitchen.'

'You take a good deal on yourself, it seems to me, Miss Parkin!' answered the landlady, a little crossly. But she was a good soul, and she hurried off, all the same, to speak with the unknown invalid.

A girl, wearing a gown of tumbled print and a straw hat, was standing half propped up against the kitchen table. She was white, livid almost, for her complexion was affected by the heat in a different way from that of the rosy Mrs. Dunlop.

'You're faint,' said the landlady kindly, seeing that the girl breathed hard, and that the perspiration stood on her forehead in large drops.

'Yes—faint—and very, very ill,' murmured the stranger. 'I've come such a long way in the broiling sun, and I was feeling unwell when I started.'

She spoke in quick gasps. Mrs. Dunlop noticed that her skirts were torn, and that pieces of briar, and here and there stems of long grass, adhered to her petticoat. Her shoes were white with dust, and jagged blades of green were hanging to one of them.

'Can you let me rest here?' said the girl, after she had drunk a glass of water, handed to her by Mrs. Dunlop, now all compassionate. 'I must get away to-night if I am better. I was going on now to the station, but I came across the fields and lost my way. All the meadows are so alike!'

'Have you come from far?'

'I hardly know—four, five miles, perhaps. But I am weak and ill, and the sun was strong.' She bowed her head down upon the wooden settle, and Mrs. Dunlop saw tears falling slowly through her fingers.

'Poor soul, you're in sad trouble!' she cried. 'You must rest here a bit, and John shall take you to the station in the dogcart. Come, cheer up, dear! Can't I help you in any way?'

The girl raised her head. She looked with a long gaze into the landlady's benevolent crimson face. 'Will you send a note for me?

You must swear to me, though, that no one else shall know where or to whom it has gone?' She spoke quickly, and with great earnestness.

'I'll do what I can to oblige,' murmured Mrs. Dunlop weakly. Whereupon the young woman drew out a sealed letter from her pocket.

'Swear to me too that you will not mention to any one that I ever took refuge here?'

The landlady hesitated. Her eyes had suddenly fallen upon the girl's left hand. She noticed a plain gold ring upon the slender third finger.

'I hardly know,' she began.

Then the young woman rose, half angrily, to her feet, grew a shade paler, and sank despairingly into her chair again.

'If I were not so ill, I'd go on now,' she whispered. 'But I should only faint by the roadside. You have a kind face — I throw myself on your pity. I am married, yes, I am, and I am flying from my husband. I put on one of the maid's dresses' — Mrs. Dunlop started—'and I came quickly away on foot. I am afraid some one saw me, but I'm not sure. I think one of his grooms did. I didn't take the main road, so I lost my way over those hot, burning fields. I swear I'll never go back to him, for nothing in this world or the next!'

'My dear, he's your wedded husband,' murmured Mrs. Dunlop feebly, thinking that some such moral observation was incumbent upon her.

'Yes, he is, God forgive him. But look here!' She tore open her dress. Across her white neck stretched a bruise, turning purple. Then she pulled up her sleeve. There was a still larger mark upon the white arm.

'Those are only some of the places where he's struck me,' said the stranger piteously. 'Now will you help me? O God! you must, and surely will?'

The tears stood in Mrs. Dunlop's eyes. 'I'll do all you ask, ma'am,' she answered in a half-extinguished voice. The girl handed her the note. It was addressed — 'T. Drax, Esq., Riverside Lodge.' Then Mrs. Dunlop got redder than ever. An idea had flashed across her brain, and she foresaw great trouble.

'I don't know, my dear; I don't know what I ought to do, I'm sure!' she cried, in perplexity and grief.

'Send it or I'll kill myself before to-morrow!' exclaimed the girl, turning still whiter. 'Yes, you shall know who I am. Ah! perhaps you guessed? My name is Edith Eddington, and I've married the greatest blackguard in the three kingdoms. O help me, as you are a good woman! Have pity on me! You don't know the things he's done and said to me!'

Mrs. Dunlop rose, hurried through the back

door, and, letter in hand, went out into the garden. A heavy boy was at work there gathering spinach. He was the deaf and dumb son of the man who looked after Mr. Dunlop's cows and horse. The landlady spoke to him on her fingers, quickly, but with an impressive air, and gave him the note. As she retraced her steps, she kept on repeating aloud—'God forgive me if it's a sin! if it's a sin! But everything's all so jumbled up in this world, the rights and the wrongs are an awful puzzle. And he struck her! Perhaps she'll suffer for that all her life, poor soul, as it is! I really don't seem for the life of me to know whose sin it may be.'

Edith Eddington was taken up the back stairs. Arrived in a spare bedroom, she threw herself upon a little sofa overlooking the cornfields, and a distant silvery glimmer of the river. There was a stretch of common land to be seen still further away, fringed by wide pastures, in which clumps of 'lambs' tongues' and tufts of rosy clover were in bloom. Beyond the river was the railway station. There is a nearer one to-day; but all this happened, you must remember, some twenty years ago. It might have been about two hours later, when the sun was no longer scorching, and the green corn began to wave gently in the cool breeze, that a man drove up in a dogcart to the

'Startled Fawn.' A very tall, very handsome young fellow, spruce and well dressed, and wearing a straw hat that threw a deep shadow over his eyes.

'Good evening, Mr. Drax,' said the ostler. Tom was well known by every one whose business led him among horses. The new-comer flung him a silver coin. 'Take the pony out,' he said, 'and don't let him bite you. He's a nasty temper sometimes.'

Then Mr. Drax went in through the front door. Mrs. Dunlop's red face peered cautiously out from the door of a private sitting-room.

'You've come quickly, Mr. Drax,' she said, and she noticed how pale his handsome face was, now that he had taken his hat off.

'Where is she?' was all that he said, speaking very slowly, as if he had great difficulty in forming even these few words. The landlady led the way up the creaking stairs. Then she waited on the landing—not that she might listen, she earnestly assured me, but only in case that she might be wanted. Just a few snatches of tremulous conversation, scattered heartbroken utterances, came to her ears through the closed doors.

'My darling, that it should come to this!' said the man's voice.

'You told me that you would be always ready, always waiting—you know that, Tom?'

sobbed the woman. 'And I don't deserve your love for me. I did marry him believing all that people said of him, and I cared for you, Tom, my darling, all the time. I did, I did! I am the weakest and wickedest of women to have treated you so, and then to come after all and spoil your life!'

'Whatever you did, however you treated me, you would for ever be my own dear little girl,' the man said in a lowered, half-dogged voice. 'Come to me now,' he said, raising his tones; 'be with me always, Edie, my own love! I will defend you, I will stay with you till the end of everything. Neither he nor any else shall part us any more.'

'Yes, yes, I will come!' She was sobbing upon his breast. 'O Tom, my dear, dear good boy, how brave and honest you have always been! It will make poor old father very angry and sad if I stay with you, I know it will, but I feel I must. What can I do? It's too great a temptation for me to fight against! When shall we go, Tom? Now—now, at once?'

'At once,' said Tom Drax. 'Your husband won't be back for some hours. We shall have a long start of him, Edie dear.'

'He is at Windsor Races, and it will be dark before he is home,' she said. The lover bent down and kissed her once again. Then he opened the door.

'Mrs. Dunlop, send my cart round to the back door. Hurry up the man, will you? there is no time to lose.' Tom Drax's voice shook a little.

The landlady went down the front stairs breathlessly enough. Through the porch a heavy dust-cloud floated in, and the sound of speech as well. A man's voice, loud and coarse in tone, said, 'So Drax is here? damn him. Ah! I thought as much.'

Mrs. Dunlop turned very pale, and moved forward to the front door. Her husband and one or two others were standing with their backs to her, confronting a tall figure, that of a person whom she knew well by sight. A burly young man, with a red, clean-shaven face, very thick lips, and narrow grey eyes. His age was about twenty-six, but he was already bald and heavy for his years. He wore extremely tight trousers, a tan-coloured coat with large buttons, and a low-crowned white hat. In his hand he held a heavy hunting crop. He was covered with dust.

'And you are not quite sure whether my lady is here or no too? You don't say so!' He smiled a little with those coarse lips of his, and there were creases at the corners of his eyes as the evil smile crept upwards. 'She means to be back, I suppose, anyhow, for dinner? Thought I was at the races, I imagine? But

I can play my little games too sometimes. Good evening, Mrs. Dunlop. You're looking uncommonly fit. We're having sultry weather, ain't we? Thanks, I'll take a gin and ginger beer, and would prefer it upstairs in a private room.'

He pushed past the group, and slowly mounted the stairway, which creaked more than ever under his fifteen-stone weight. Arrived at the top, he laughed aloud a harsh, metallic laugh, and cracked his hunting crop still more noisily.

'Hallo, my lady! Hope you're rested by this time? Won't you come and have a chat and a whisky-and-soda with me before we start home?'

There was a faint cry from one of the rooms that sounded like the scream of a startled and wounded animal. Lord Eddington laughed again, crossed the landing, and knocked loudly at the door whence the sound proceeded. There was no answer. He tried the door handle.

'Locked, by ——,' said he, and he kicked at the panels with his great boots.

There was a rustle within, and a woman's voice said piteously—

'Tom, darling, don't go. Can't we get down through the window? Better to die that way!'

'Go back, Edith, and stand in the corner,'

said Tom Drax. Then he flung open the door, and stood with folded arms, his handsome face quite pale, his dark eyes burning, his lips set tight. Mr. and Mrs. Dunlop and the barmaid and several guests, one and all scared and quite silent, were standing down below listening and terrified.

'You damned blackguard!' said Lord Eddington. 'I heard, you see, that the little bird had flown from one of my faithful retainers. But you're just a little bit too late! And I've come to give you the —— horsewhipping that man ever had.'

'You've come for your wife too, I suppose?' said Tom Drax calmly, though his eyes blazed what he felt, 'and you won't get her; no, not if all the devils in hell were at your side. You shan't take her from me again! Do you hear, you scoundrel? You've struck her, yes, you did, you infernal brute, on her mouth and on her neck! You've insulted her before your servants and the curs you call your friends. And, by God, you will not move a step further towards her unless it's over my body!'

'Take that, you cursed, swaggering fool!' said the other man. And he struck Tom Drax with the whip right across the mouth, till the blood started out. The bookmaker was the stronger man of the two, and in far better condition. He returned the blow vigorously with his fist, and Lord Eddington reeled backward. Then the people below heard a shriek, and Edith ran across the room, on to the landing, her fragile arms outstretched, as she tried to separate the men. Eddington caught one of her little hands in his iron grasp, then the other, and forced her down upon her knees, till Tom Drax closed savagely with the husband of the woman he loved, and tried to hurl him to the ground. Mrs. Dunlop feebly screamed below. At length Edith staggered to her feet, and clutching Eddington round his waist, looked up eloquently at him. He turned his purple face loweringly towards her, and mumbling at her some of the epithets of which he was a master, he disengaged one of her hands and roughly pushed her from him. The three had unconsciously drawn near the head of the staircase in their movements, and when he hurled her backwards she lost her balance. With one loud cry of fear and anguish she fell down all the first flight of oak steps, striking her head sharply against an old iron-bound chest that stood upon the landing. Then she lay still. A narrow red stream trickled slowly from her forehead over the polished boards.

'You've killed her,' said Tom Drax, quite in a whisper, with clenched teeth, loosening his hold as he spoke, 'and you'll go to hell for this whether or no I send you there.'

They lifted Edith's senseless body and bore it into the bedroom overlooking the green corn and the sweet clover-fields, shining all rosy under the lowering sun.

. . . . . .

'She did not die!' I said, for Mrs. Dunlop had grown husky, and was mopping her eyes and face.

'Die, sir! Perhaps it would have been better so. But how can we poor mortals tell? Week after week she lay in that room up above there, till the poppies and corn-cockles faded, and the wheat and barley grew golden, and was carried in sheaves away. And of all that she knew nothing. It was injury to the brain, and often she used to scream out loud and cry, and wring her hands, 'Don't hit me, Charlie! You've hurt my chest so! I shall die of a cancer!' she would say; or, 'Tom, Tom, I am waiting, darling; I know I shan't live much longer if you don't soon come.' For, dear soul, she didn't know how often Mr. Drax really was there, holding her poor hot hands in his, and putting ice upon her head, and nursing her like a mother would. Many's the race-meeting where they must have missed his face, for he wouldn't ever go away while she was in danger. And he brought his sister to help to nurse her too. Lord Eddington! Oh no, he never once came near her, but went right away, somewhere abroad I've heard tell. He didn't try, not he, for a divorce, for he couldn't have got it; and they say when he came back to England, he was for ever living in low company, and drinking, and cursing, and swearing, till he died some ten years since. And his poor wife—why—ah, dear me, no, her senses did not come back ever again. It was a cruel thing, wasn't it, to bear? Tom Drax, he says to me, "I shall keep her with me, Mrs. Dunlop, always, so long as I live. She will come to my father's house, and we'll all do what we can, but I fear it's but little," so he says. Poor young man! His heart was about broke. They do say, these many long years, for all he's such a handsome fellow still, that he never so much as looks at a woman. Strange, ain't it? You'd hardly believe that, sir? He just waits on, and hopes, and hopes that poor Lady Eddington will get well, and then he says he'll marry her. When her father, old Brunner, died, the Draxes bought his house on the river, that nice red one, sir, with the ivy growing all over it; you may see them often of an evening out boating. Perhaps they'll be having a row to-night as you go back; it's quite likely. There's old Mr. Drax and his daughter, and his two nieces, and Lady Eddington and Tom all living there.'

The sun was low now, and the green corn-sheaths were bathed in an atmosphere of pale, pure gold, these same quiet fields over which a frightened woman had hurried despairingly some twenty years ago to the sign of the 'Startled Fawn.' I rose, thanked my hostess heartily for her story, said good-night, and drove away towards the station. As I passed across the bridge, at the corner of which stands an ivy-covered red house, I stopped for a moment, and looked down at the clear river in which every willow leaf was reflected, till the stream appeared an expanse of luminous green. I heard the plashing of sculls, and a boat came towards the landing-place. A tall man, of about forty-five years old, who I saw had curly dark hair and broad shoulders, pushed back his straw hat, and the evening glow shone full upon his handsome face. It was a familiar one to me, for I had often seen Tom Drax before now at Newmarket, and Epsom, and Doncaster. He shipped his sculls, and his companions prepared to get out. They comprised two pretty girls dressed in white flannel, and a middle-aged woman, wearing rather creased blue serge. I noticed that her hair was grey, and that it looked rough and untidy under her shady hat. Tom Drax gave her his hand, and one of the girls joined him in helping her to leave the boat. All of a sudden a fish jumped close to the group. The elder grey-haired woman started, pointed with her finger to the bubbles in the river, and laughed aloud in a foolish, wild way. And she went on laughing still, and pointing at the water, as she stood upon the steps of the landing-place. I heard her curious, unmirthful tones ringing out again and again as the party went slowly up the slope towards the red house, Tom Drax gently leading the afflicted woman by the arm. When they reached the velvet sward of the lawn they turned round once more. Tom's kind, handsome face was downbent towards his companion, who was still laughing, but more quietly now, as if at some jest known only to herself. I touched my pony lightly with the whip, and drove on quickly, and I found, as I drew near the station, that my eyes were dim and wet, and that I saw the waving green of the corn-fields, the lilac mallow clusters in the hedgerows, and the smoke of my approaching train, as a landscape darkened and blurred by an overhanging mist.

IN THE INFIRMARY

The nurse was moving slowly through the dimly lighted ward. On one arm she carried a huge bunch of shining holly. She paused at every narrow bed, and fastened a cluster of the glossy leaves and blood-red berries against the yellow-washed wall, just over the head of the recumbent patient. Some of these sick people smiled up at her half-wearily, and thanked her. Others again seemed hardly to notice her well-intentioned effort at decoration. A few—these had contorted features and drawn cheeks—lay back moaning, as if in pain. When the nurse came to where James Vincent lay, he was looking as usual straight out in front of him, with a hopeless stare in his great dark eyes. She stopped a moment longer than usual by his bed.

'Are you feeling any worse this evening?' she asked in a calm, conventional tone, that was as far from being totally unfeeling as it was from expressing real sympathy.

'Thank God, I believe I am,' said the man sharply, still staring at the opposite wall.

'Well, I must say, Vincent, you don't show overmuch gratitude for kindness,' answered the woman snappishly, passing on to the next bed. Old Ben, who was its occupant, and afflicted with softening of the brain, burst out into a sort of prolonged chuckle as he touched the glossy holly with his wrinkled hands.

'This 'minds me,' he said confidentially, ' of Christmas at the old place. 'I used to stick them branches, I did, into the corners of Squire's pew, and over the parson's head, too, that I did!' Benny looked round to see if any one else was listening. But the other occupants of the ward were tired of the Squire, and indeed of most of Ben's reminiscences. Seeing that no one was attending, the old man relapsed into a mortified silence.

His neighbour, James Vincent, turned towards him with a half-smile on his white face.

'Those must have been great days at the Hall, Benny,' he said in a low, gasping voice.

'I should *rayther* think so! The old Squire, why, he used to send us all beef and a great big slice of puddin'; and me and my brothers, 'im as was killed at Inkerman and t'other who was blown up in the mine, we went out singin' with the waits. And one Christmas Eve—'e was a 'ot-tempered man, was Squire (though he'd a grand voice, and read the lessons reg'lar), 'e got into a towering rage, and said 'e wouldn't stand this blasted row, and if 'e didn't fetch out his gun, and by —— if 'e didn't pepper us pretty smart on the legs! Me and my brothers, we did 'oller!' This anecdote, having been related on an average some three times a week, had entirely ceased to thrill Ben's fellow-sufferers. But he went on softly chuckling over it to himself, almost until the nurse had finished her task. She stood in the middle of the room, regarding the result of her efforts with some pride. Her face wore a fixed expression of self-righteous resignation on which she piqued herself. She had been deprived, owing to the illness of another nurse, of her accustomed Christmas holiday; and although she honestly intended to do her duty by the patients, she was equally determined that they should be aware that she found but little pleasure in performing it. Doubtless this knowledge did not tend towards creating a feeling of joviality in her particular ward of the workhouse infirmary. In spite of the row of gas-burners, and a tolerable fire, the room felt damp and cold. Outside a heavy fog hung over the sea, and chilled the bodies of people who were doing their Christmas shopping. Greasy layers of mud clung to the petticoats of tired women tramping along with heavy baskets on their arms. Here and there a group of sailors, who always, somehow, look cheerful on shore, passed along laughing and jesting. But the greater part of the landsmen were blue and pinched, and not overmuch disposed to merriment. Heavy drops fell off the railings on to the sticky pavement, and the shroud-like mist to seaward seemed to grow every moment thicker and greyer. On still evenings like this the sound of the warning bell, hanging on a treacherous rock out at sea, could be heard very plainly in the workhouse. James Vincent lay awake listening to its plaintive knell. He liked the stormy nights far better, when the windows rattled, and the great waves came tearing and rushing towards the sea wall in a furious phalanx. This stillness, broken only by the melancholy clang of the bell, was terribly dreary, and matched the unbroken, monotonous pain of his own thoughts. He was too weak to read, although there were several books at his elbow.

The chaplain, an inexperienced but amiable young man, had failed to make much of James Vincent. He had started at the first sound of the sick man's voice—at the pure intonation, which showed him that the speaker was a man as educated and refined as he himself, and he had felt interested, and anxious to be of use, but he could never get Vincent to talk, much less to confide in him.

'Ah! I see you have got Shelley's poem,'

and James Thomson's. A terrible pessimist, the latter,' said the clergyman tentatively.

'He was,' answered Vincent.

'Would you care for any other more— more cheerful books, or some, perhaps, of a—a religious tendency?' blurted out the chaplain, with a slight blush. He felt that those dark eyes that were fixed on him shone with a half-sarcastic smile in their depths.

'I have all the books I want, thanks; and I don't ever care to be read to,' answered James Vincent, not uncivilly, in his calm, well-modulated tones.

The chaplain made one more unsuccessful effort.

'I was wondering if—if you had any friends who—who —— I meant if you would like me to write or do anything, I—I should be so glad if it were in my power, you know?'

'You are very kind,' said James Vincent, in a harder voice. 'I have no friends.'

The clergyman nervously fingered the little volume of Shelley, coughed, and went on his way to talk to the more forthcoming patient with the bandaged head, and the old man with the grey beard who groaned so much in one corner, and whom the doctor said was never quite out of pain; and the boy with the hot flush on his cheeks, and the disagreeable-looking person in the other corner bed with an evil, sodden face, and red-rimmed eyes.

Just once before this particular Christmas Eve, when the bells were ringing peals all through the foggy town, and the mist hung so heavily over the sea, James Vincent had seemed to brighten up ever so little. It was after he had been reading a local newspaper. He then asked for pen and ink, and told the nurse that he wished to write a letter. He was now far too weak to guide a pen over the sheets; on that day he had acquired a sudden accession of strength. He had written his first and last letter since coming to the workhouse, and smiled as he hunted in his box and found a fragment of sealing wax, with which he had fastened the shabby envelope. The letter was addressed (the nurse noticed with some surprise) to somebody living in the fashionable suburb of the seaport. These were the words which it contained—

'I see in the list of visitors that *you* are actually here! You whom I have thought of every day, every hour almost, during these past years, in spite of all my sins, all my folly. I don't think, somehow, either, that you can have quite forgotten, have you? You used to tell me in chaff when we walked under the red and yellow trees by the mere, and when we sat together in the firelight, that if I went on with the life I was leading I should end in the workhouse. Funny, wasn't it, your saying that? Did you believe, dear, that it was a true prophecy? For now I *am* actually here at last (for a very little time more), in a grim infirmary ward, surrounded with many other poor wrecks of humanity, most of them far more blameless than I, and none perhaps so despairing. The doctor and the parson (a well-meaning ass that last) would like to help me if they could; but what should they do for a man who has ceased to hope, to believe, almost to wish? Yes, a man who is dead to all desires but one, and that is to look for a moment before he dies on the face of a woman who once loved him. Yes, who did care. You did? I know you must have done so, or you would not have looked at me with such tenderness and sweetness, and talked as you used to do. And your voice; I can hear it now ever so plainly, echoing all down this dreary room; between the pauses of the bell that rings out at sea your voice trembles. . . . What a fool I am! You have most likely quite forgotten it all, or hate to think of it; and, of course, I do want you to forget, my dear; I do, indeed, and to be always happy. But, you see, I am here only for such a short time more, and if you were to be kind and to come—— Oh, let me think that you

will, if only for a minute, and I swear to you
that I will never, never, after that, trouble you
again! No . . .

> "Dear, I look from my hiding-place.
> Are you still so fair, have you still the eyes?
>
> . . . . .
>
> I knew you once; but in Paradise,
> If we meet, I will pass, nor turn my face."'

The letter was signed with initials, but they were not those of the name by which the writer was known in the infirmary ward.

Christmas Eve was closing in. James Vincent still looked blankly in front of him sometimes. Then he would shut his eyes. He breathed all the time terribly quickly. The man in the corner was tossing from side to side and groaning, old Benny was fast asleep, dreaming of past and more jocund Christmastides, and the boy with the bright eyes coughed his hard, dry cough at frequent intervals.

'There's a young person asking to see you, Vincent,' said the nurse.

He heard her voice as if in a dream, but a wild thrill—was it a pang of joy again?—shook his wasted body. Meanwhile, somebody, whose boots creaked, drew near the bedside. It was a short girl, obviously belonging to the class of servants familiarly known as 'generals.' She was dressed in an ill-fitting black jacket, and wore a necktie of crude magenta and a hat adorned with the brightest of blue feathers. She tightly clutched several untidy parcels in her bare, red hands. Her thin cheeks were even more crimson than her cold fingers.

James Vincent felt a long stab of agony and disappointment, and then as if an icy grasp held him fast. At the same time, a sense of the bitter irony of life almost made him smile. He had half expected — what a damned fool he was, he thought—some one richly dressed, with a clear skin and great grey eyes. A woman who used to speak in a low, musical voice, and who would lay a little white hand in his, while she smiled at him. And it was only the poor, grotesque figure of Molly, the servant-girl at his last lodgings, who stood shyly in front of him, flaming more and more under his gaze.

'I thought you wouldn't mind me coming!' she gasped. 'Missis 'av kep' me pretty hard at it; but it's Christmas Eve, and the children are out, and they don't want no supper. They've gone to see the old gentleman's brother, and I thought, you being so ill, you might like—I've 'eard they don't give you much up 'ere—something nice for your tea. So I—I brought these.' She trembled as she undid her parcels, and laid a tin of potted lobster, one of corned beef, and a bag of ginger-bread upon the creased check-quilt. Something with a bit of taste, you see,' said Molly, half apologetically, but with a subdued sense of pride within.

James Vincent had recovered his composure, and smiled at her. 'You are a kind little girl, my dear,' he said gently.

Something in the tone of his voice struck her very painfully.

'Lor! you *do* look bad! P'raps you can't even eat them things!' she cried, the tears suddenly welling up into her eyes. 'I thought you'd fancy the lobster. Do it hurt you so much, then, to speak? Well, just you smell these, Mr. Vincent. I brought them for you, too. They're pretty, aren't they?'

She shyly pushed a bunch of half-withered yellow chrysanthemums into his wasted hands. A spasm that was made up of pain, and pity, and gratitude shook the man a little as he touched the flowers.

'You shouldn't spend so much on me,' he whispered, for he knew that Molly's wages were eighteenpence a week, and that she had been in sore need of new boots, and of a warm coat, when he had lodged at her master's.

'I wanted to come, you see,' said the girl, in a choked voice, 'and bring you a bit of something to cheer you up just for Christmas. It seems so lonely here in this bare old place, and you used always to speak so nice and kind to me, and you gave me that stuff for the toothache and all.'

She was crying quite fast now. Vincent held her chapped red hand in his long, white ones for a moment.

'God bless you, my dear,' he said. 'I am not worth crying for. I am not really. Believe me, I thank you more than I can tell you. It isn't much use'—here he tried to smile—'wishing each other "A Merry Christmas," is it? But still it's nice not to be quite forgotten. And wherever I am going, Molly, I don't believe, if I remember anything, that I shall forget you.'

She turned her head sharply away, and walked quite slowly down the ward. The man with the sodden face laughed a little as he looked at her, and made a joke about her blue feather. But she did not even hear him. Nor did she know that a pair of large sad eyes followed her grotesque little figure until it disappeared through the door. Then they closed again. That night was a bad one for James Vincent. His dark head slipped lower and lower down in his bed; his breathing came quicker and quicker, and in hard, painful gasps. He scarcely knew that the doctor came in once or twice, or that the nurse was yawning by his side at intervals for long hours. Towards morning, when the Christmas bells from all the neighbouring churches jostled each other in

IN THE INFIRMARY

merry chimes, he seemed a little better. At eleven o'clock the chaplain entered and read a few prayers. These over, the nurse, in a gloomy voice, for she was still feeling injured as she thought of her absent home-circle, with its attractions in the form of mince-pies and snap-dragon, gave the patients the inappropriate and conventional salutation that she considered proper to the season. Merriment was represented by a plum-pudding and an extra allowance of tough beef for dinner in the ward, and by the man with the sodden face, who was prompted to be facetious. But all these things seemed blurred and unreal to James Vincent. He did not notice that a servant in livery came to the door and stood talking to the nurse, or that the latter drew near him a few minutes afterwards with her arms full of white and blue parcels. Old Benny, however, looked up, excited and curious.

'See 'im there with the cockade in 'is 'at!' he cried admiringly, pointing to the vanishing form of the footman. 'That 'minds me of our Squire. He had three of them chaps, and when Mr. Guy came of age they 'ad their 'eads all whitened over with flour! I see 'em, I did, when the Squire spoke to us and cracked 'is jokes out on the steps. That I did.'

'Well, Vincent, just try and look up! See what's here for you,' said the nurse, more softly than usual. For she knew that she would not have many more opportunities of addressing this unfriendly and refractory patient. 'It's some tea and sugar, and I don't know what else. Oh! yes, here's some nice jelly and beautiful Brand's extract for you from a lady.'

Vincent vainly tried to raise himself. Then he scowled at the nurse.

'From a lady?' he whispered.

'Yes, it looks as if there's still some charity left in the world,' said the nurse, with more conviction than tact. She glanced at the sick man, and realised that his face was a complete mystery. It wore an expression of bitter rage, of loathing and despair.

'Damn her and her charity!' he said, in a voice the clearness and firmness of which astonished the nurse fully as much as that terrible look in his eyes. 'Take them to Benny,' he continued, still speaking quite loud, 'and put those other things that came yesterday by me. Ah! you've let the flowers die!' He spoke fiercely, and tried to reach the withered chrysanthemums. Then he turned his face away and buried it in the tumbled pillow. Towards evening the doctor came in again, and looked gravely at Vincent. Then he spoke low to the nurse. He went away, only to come back presently with another and older physician. They two and the nurse stood for some moments in silence by Vincent, whose breath came in terribly laboured and painful gasps. As they watched him, they heard the sound of laughter and cheerful young voices floating in from the distant door. 'Dear me, it's the ladies who was to have come and sung carols to the patients, sir,' said the nurse.

'Not now, it's impossible,' answered the doctor sharply. He walked towards the entrance, and spoke to a group of smiling girls who were passing in.

'I am afraid we must put off the singing,' he said, 'until to-morrow perhaps.'

The sodden-faced man looked up with curiosity and a disagreeable grin. Old Benny murmured something in a loud whisper to his neighbour.

A few of the patients seemed interested, one or two a little sorry, some indifferent. They were accustomed enough to episodes of this kind. They thought that they would have liked to hear the carols. It would have been a change, and the days were very long.

'Shall I tell the chaplain to come to him?' said the young doctor.

'What's the use?' said the older man. 'You can see for yourself that he wouldn't understand a word now.'

And the three drew a large screen round James Vincent's bed.

THE SPECTRE OF THE REAL

By THOMAS HARDY AND FLORENCE HENNIKER

CHAPTER I

A CERTAIN March night of this present 'waning age' had settled down upon the woods and the park and the parapets of Ambrose Towers. The harsh stable-clock struck a quarter to ten. Thereupon a girl in light evening attire and wraps came through the entrance-hall, opened the front door and the small wrought-iron gate beyond it which led to the terrace, and stepped into the moonlight. Such a person, such a night, and such a place were unexceptionable materials for a scene in that poetical drama of two which the world has often beheld, which leads up to a contract that causes a slight sinking in the poetry, and a perceptible lack of interest in the play.

She moved so quietly that the alert birds resting in the great cedar-tree never stirred. Gliding across its funereal shadow over a smooth plush of turf, as far as to the Grand Walk whose pebbles shone like the floor-stones of the Apocalyptic City, she paused and looked back at the old brick walls—red in the daytime, sable now—at the shrouded mullions, the silhouette of the tower, though listening rather than seeing seemed her object in coming to the pause. The clammy wings of a bat brushed past her face, startling her and making her shiver a little. The stamping of one or two horses in their stalls surprised her by its distinctness and isolation. The servants' offices were on the other side of the house, and the lady who, with the exception of the girl on the terrace, was its sole occupant, was resting on a sofa behind one of the curtained windows. So Rosalys went on her way unseen, trod the margin of the lake, and plunged into the distant shrubberies.

The clock had reached ten. As the last stroke of the hour rang out a young man scrambled down the sunk fence bordering the pleasure-ground, leapt the iron railing within, and joined the girl who stood awaiting him. In the half-light he could not see how her full underlip trembled, or the fire of joy that kindled in her eyes. But perhaps he guessed from daylight experiences, since he passed his arm round her shoulders with assurance, and kissed her ready mouth many times. Her head still resting against his arm, they walked towards a bench, the rough outlines of which were touched at one end only by the moon-rays. At the dark end the pair sat down.

'I cannot come again,' said the girl.

'Oh?' he vaguely returned. 'This is new. What has happened? I thought you said your mother supposed you to be working at your Harmony, and would never imagine our meeting here?' The voice sounded just a trifle hard for a lover's.

'No, she would not. And I still detest deceiving her. I would do it for no one but you, Jim. But what I meant was this: I feel that it can all lead to nothing. Mother is not a bit more worldly than most people, but she naturally does not want her only child to marry a man who has nothing but the pay of an officer in the Line to live upon. At her death (you know she has only a life-interest here) I should have to go away unless my uncle, who succeeds, chose to take me to stay with him. I have no fortune of my own beyond a mere pittance. Two hundred a year.'

Jim's reply was something like a sneer at the absent lady: 'You may as well add to the practical objection the sentimental one—that she wouldn't allow you to change your fine old crusted name for mine, which is merely the older one of the little freeholder turned out of this spot by your ancestor when he came.'

'Dear, dear Jim, don't say those horrid things! As if *I* had ever even thought of that for a moment!'

He shook her hand off impatiently, and walked out into the moonlight. Certainly, as far as physical outline went, he might have been the direct product of a line of Paladins or hereditary Crusaders. He was tall, straight of limb, with an aquiline nose, and a mouth fitfully scornful. Rosalys sat almost motionless watching him. There was no mistaking the ardour of her feelings; her power over him seemed to be lessened by his consciousness of his influence upon the lower and weaker side of her nature. It gratified him as a man to feel it; and though she was beautiful enough to satisfy the senses of the critical, there was perhaps something of contempt interwoven with his love. His victory had been too easy, too complete.

'Dear Jim, you are not going to be vexed? It really isn't my fault that I can't come out here again! Mother will be downstairs to-morrow, and then she might take it into her head to look at any time into the schoolroom and see how the Harmony gets on.'

'And you are going off to London soon?' said Jim, still speaking gloomily.

'I am afraid so. But couldn't you come there too? I know your leave is not up for a great many weeks?'

He was silent for longer than she had ever known him at these times. Rosalys left her seat on the bench and threw her arms impulsively round him.

'I *can't* go away unless you will come to London when we do, Jim!'

'I will; but on one condition.'

'What condition? You frighten me!'

'That you will marry me when I do join you there.'

The quick breath that heaved in Rosalys ebbed silently, and she leant on the rustic bench with one hand, a trembling being apparent in her garments.

'You really—mean it, Jim, darling?'

He swore that he did; that life was quite unendurable to him as he then experienced it. When she was once his wife, nothing would come between them; but, of course, the marriage need not be known for a time—indeed, must not. He could not take her abroad. The climate of Burmah would be too trying for her; and, besides, they really would not have enough to live upon.

'Couldn't we get on as other people do?' said Rosalys, trying not to cry at these arguments. 'I am so tired of concealment, and I don't like to marry privately! It seems to me, much as I love being with you, that there is a sort of—well—vulgarity in our clandestine meetings as we now enjoy them. Therefore, how should I ever have strength enough to hide the fact of my being your wife, to face my mother day after day with the shadow of this secret between us?'

For all answer Jim kissed her, and stroked her silky, brown curls.

'I suppose I shall end in agreeing with you —I always do!' she said, her mouth quivering. 'Though I *can* be very dogged and obstinate too, Jim! Do you know that all my governesses have said I was the most stubborn child they ever came across? But then, in that case, my temper must be really aroused. You have never seen me as I am when angry. Perhaps, Jim, you would get to hate me?'

She looked at him wistfully with her wet eyes.

'I shall never cease to love you desperately, as I do now!' declared the young man. 'How lovely you look, little Rosalys, with that one moonbeam making your forehead like pure white marble. But time is passing. You must go back, my darling, I'm afraid. And you won't fail me in London? I shall make all the plans. Good-bye—good-bye!'

One clinging, intermittent kiss; and then from the shadow in which he stood Jim watched her light figure passing the lake, and hurrying along in the shelter of the yew hedges towards the great house, asleep under reaching deeps of sky, and the vacant gaze of the round white moon.

CHAPTER II

WHEN clouds are iron-grey above the prim drab houses, and a hard east wind blows flakes of dust, stable-straws, scraps of soiled newspaper, and sharp pieces of grit into the eyes of foot-passengers, a less inviting and romantic dwelling-spot than Belgrave Road can hardly be experienced.

But the Prince's daughter of the Canticles, emerging from her palace to see the vine flourish and the pomegranates bud forth with her Beloved, could not have looked more unconscious of grime than Rosalys Ambrose as she came down the steps of one of the tall houses in the aforesaid respectable place of residence. Her cheeks were hotly pink, her eyes shining, her lips parted. Having once made up her mind, 'qualms of prudence, pride and pelf,' had died within her passionate little heart. After to-day she would belong absolutely to Jim, be his alone, through all the eternities, as it seemed; and of what account was anything else in the world? The entirely physical character of his affection for her, and perhaps of hers for him, was an unconjectured element herein which might not render less transitory the most transitory of sweet things. Thus hopefully she stepped out of the commonplace home that would, in one sense, be hers no more

The raw wind whistled up the street, and deepened the colour on her face. She was plainly dressed in grey, and wore a rather thick veil, natural to the dusty day; it could not however conceal the sparkle of her eyes; veils, even thick ones, happily, never do. Hailing a hansom, she told the driver to take her to the corner of the Embankment.

In the midst of her preoccupation she noticed as the cab turned the corner out of Belgrave Road that the bony chestnut-horse went lame. Rosalys was superstitious as well as tender-hearted, and she deemed that some stroke of ill-luck might befall if she drove to be married behind a suffering animal. She alighted and paid off the man, and in her excitement gave him three times his fare. Hurrying forward on foot, she heard her name called, and received a cordial greeting from a tall man with grey whiskers, in whom she recognised Mr. Durrant, Jim's father. It occurred to her for a second that he might have discovered the plot and have lain in wait to prevent it. However, he spoke in his usual half-respectful, half-friendly tones, not noticing her frightened face. Mr Durrant was a busy man. Besides holding several very important land-agencies in the county where Rosalys lived, he had business in the City to transact at times. He explained to Miss Ambrose that some urgent affairs he was supervising for a client of his, Lord Parkhurst, had now brought him up to London for a few weeks.

'Lord Parkhurst is away?' she asked, to say something. 'I hear of him sometimes through his uncle Colonel Lacy.'

'Yes. A thorough sailor. Mostly afloat,' Mr. Durrant replied. 'Well—we're rather out of the way in Porchester Terrace. Otherwise my wife would be so pleased if you would come to tea, Miss Ambrose! My son Jim, lazy young beggar, is up here now too—going to plays and parties. Well, well, it's natural he should like to amuse himself before he leaves for Burmah, poor boy. Are you looking for a hansom? Yes! Hi!' and he waved his stick.

'Thank you so much,' said Miss Ambrose. 'And I will tell mamma where you and Mrs. Durrant are staying.'

She was surprised at her own composure. Her unconscious father-in-law elect helped her into the cab, took off his hat, and walked rapidly away. Rosalys felt her heart stand still when she drew up at the place of meeting. She saw Jim, very blooming, and very well dressed, awaiting her, outwardly calm, at any rate. He jumped into her vehicle, and they drove on City-wards.

'You are only ten minutes late, dearest,' he said. 'Do you know, I was half afraid you might have failed me at the last moment?'

'You don't believe it, Jim!'

'Well, I sometimes think I ought not to expect you to keep engagements with me so honestly as you do. Good, brave little Rosalys!'

They moved on through the press of struggling omnibuses, gigantic vans, covered carts, and foot-passengers who darted at imminent risk of their lives amid the medley of wheels, horses, and shouting drivers. The noise jarred Rosalys' head, and she began to be feverishly anxious.

The church stood in the neighbourhood of a great meat-market, and the pavement was crowded by men in blue linen blouses, their clothes sprinkled with crimson stains. The young girl gave a shiver of disgust.

'How revolting it must be to have a butcher for a husband! They can't have hearts like other men. . . . What a gloomy part of London this is to be married in, Jim!'

'Ah—yes! Everything looks gloomy with the east wind blowing. Now, here we are! Jump out, little woman!'

He handed money to the driver, who went off with the most cursory thoughts of the part that he had played in this little excursion of a palpitating pair into the unknown.

'Jimmy, darling; oughtn't you, or one of us, to have lived here for fifteen days?' she said, as they entered the fine old Norman porch, to which she was quite blind in her preoccupation.

Durrant laughed. 'I have declared that I did,' he answered coolly. 'I hope in the circumstances that it's a forgivable lie. Cheer up, Rosalys; don't all of a sudden look so solemn!'

There were tears in her eyes. The gravity of the step she was about to take had begun to frighten her.

They had some time to wait before the clergyman condescended to come out of the vestry and perform the ceremony which was to unite her to Jim. Two or three other couples were also in the church on the same errand: a haggard woman in a tawdry white bonnet, hanging on to the arm of a short, crimson-faced man, who had evidently been replenishing his inside with gin to nerve himself to the required pitch for the ordeal; a girl with a coarse, hard face, accompanied by a slender youth in shabby black; a tall man of refined aspect, in very poor clothes, whose hollow cough shook his thin shoulders and chest, and told his bride that her happiness, such as it was, would probably last but the briefest space.

Rosalys glanced absently at the beautiful building, with its Norman apse and transverse arches of horse-shoe form, and the massive curves and cushion-capitals that supported the tower-end; the whole impression left by the church being one of singular harmony, loveliness, and above all, repose—which struck even her by its great contrast with her experiences just then. As the clergyman emerged from the vestry a shaft of sunlight smote the altar, touched the quaint tomb where the founder of the building lay in his dreamless sleep, and quivered on the darned clothes of the consumptive bridegroom.

Jim and Rosalys moved forward, and then the light shone for a moment too upon his yellow hair and handsome face. To the woman who loved him it seemed that 'from the crown of his head even to the sole of his foot there was no blemish in him.'

The curate looked sharply at the four couples; angrily, Rosalys fancied, at her. But it was only because the east wind had given him an acute toothache that his gaze was severe, and his reading spiritless.

The four couples having duly contracted their inviolable unities, and slowly gone their ways through the porch, Jim and Rosalys adjourned to a fashionable hotel on the Embankment, where in a room all to themselves they had luncheon, over which Rosalys presided with quite a housewifely air.

'When shall I see you again?' he said, as he put her into a cab two or three hours later on in the afternoon.

'You must arrange all that, Jim. Somehow I feel so depressed, so dreadfully sad now, all of a sudden! Have I been wicked? I don't know!'

Her tone changed, as she met his passionate gaze, and she said very low with a lump in her throat—

'O my dear darling! I care for nothing in the whole wide world, now that I belong to you!'

CHAPTER III

THE London weeks went by with all their commonplaces, all their novelties. Mr. Durrant, senior, had finished his urgent business, and returned to his square and uninteresting country house. But Jim lingered on in town, although conscious of some subtle change in himself and his view of things. He and Rosalys met whenever it was possible, which was pretty frequently. Often they contrived to do so at hastily arranged luncheons and teas at hotels or restaurants; sometimes, when Mrs. Ambrose was suddenly called away, at Jim's own rooms. Sometimes they adventured to queer suburban coffee-houses.

In the lapse of these weeks the twain began somehow to lose a little of their zest for each other's society. Jim himself was aware of it before he had yet discovered that something of the same disappointment was dulling her heart too. On his own side it was the usual lowering of the fire—the slackening of a man's passion for a woman when she becomes his property. On hers it was a more mixed feeling. No doubt her love for Jim had been of but little higher quality than his for her. She had thoroughly abandoned herself to his good looks, his recklessness, his eagerness; and, now that the novelty of wifedom was past, her fervour also began to burn itself down. But beyond, above, this, the concealment of her marriage was repugnant to Rosalys. When the rapture of the early meetings had died away she began to loathe the sordid deceit which these involved; the secretly despatched letters, the unavoidably brazen lies to her mother, who, if she attached overmuch importance to money and birth, yet loved her daughter in all good faith and simplicity. Then once or twice Jim was late at their interviews. He seemed indifferent and preoccupied. His manner stung Rosalys into impatient utterance at the end of a particular meeting in which this mood was unduly prominent.

'You forget all I have given up for you!'

she cried. 'You make a fool of me in allowing me to wait here for you. It is humiliating and vulgar. I hate myself for behaving as I do!'

'The renunciations are not all on your side,' he answered caustically. 'You forget all that the loss of his freedom means to a man!'

Her heart swelled, and she had great difficulty in keeping back her tears. But she took refuge in sullenness.

'Unfortunately we can't undo our folly!' she murmured. 'You will have to make the best of it as well as I. I suppose the awakening to a sense of our idiocy was bound to come sooner or later. But—I didn't think it would come so soon. Jim, look at me! Are you really angry. Don't, for God's sake, go and leave me like this!'

He was walking slowly towards the great iron gate leading out of Kensington Gardens, a dogged cast on his now familiar countenance.

'Don't make a scene in public, for Heaven's sake, Rosalys!'

Feeling that he had spoken too brutally, he suddenly paused and changed.

'I am sorry, little woman, if I was cross! But things have combined to harass me lately. Of course we won't part from one another in anger.'

Jim glanced at her straight profile with its

full underlip and firmly curved chin, at the lashes on either lid, and the glossy brown hair twisted in coils under her hat. But the sight of this loveliness, now all his own, failed to arouse the old emotions. He simply contemplated her approvingly from an artistic point of view.

They had reached the gateway, and she placed her hand on his arm.

'Good-bye. When shall we next meet? To-day is Tuesday. Shall it be Friday?'

'I am afraid I must go out of London on Thursday for a day or two. I'll write, dear. Let me call a hansom.'

She thanked him in a cold voice again, and with a last handshake, and a smile that hovered on sorrow, left him and drove away towards Belgravia.

Once or twice later on they met; the next interview being shorter and sadder perhaps than the last. The one that followed it ended in bitterness.

'This had better be our long good-bye, I suppose?' said she.

'Perhaps it had. . . . You seem to be always looking out for causes of reproach, Rosalys. I don't know what has come over you.'

'It is *you* who have changed!' she cried, with a little stamp. 'And you are by far the most to blame of us two. You forget that I should never have contemplated marriage as a possibility! You have made me lie to my mother, do things of which I am desperately ashamed, and now you don't attempt to disguise your weariness of me!'

It was Jim's turn to lose his temper now. 'You forget that *you* gave me considerable encouragement! Most girls would not have come out again and again to surreptitious meetings with a man who was in love with them—girls brought up as you have been!'

She started as in a spasm. A momentary remorse seized him. He realised that he had been betrayed into speaking as no man of kindly good-feeling could speak. He made a tardy, scarcely gracious apology, and they parted. A few days afterwards he wrote a letter full of penitence for having hurt her, and she answered almost affectionately. But each knew that their short-lived romance was dead as the wind-flowers that had blossomed at its untimely birth.

CHAPTER IV

In August this pair of disappointed people met once more amid their old surroundings. Perhaps their enforced absence from one another gave at first some zest to their reunion. Jim was at times tender, and like his former self;

Rosalys, if sad and subdued, less sullen and reproachful than she had been in London.

Mrs. Ambrose had fallen into delicate health, and her daughter was in consequence able to dispose of her time outside the house as she wished. The moonlight meetings with Jim were discontinued; but husband and wife went for long strolls sometimes in the remoter nooks of the park, through winding walks in the distant shrubberies, and down paths hidden by high yew hedges from intruding eyes that might look with suspicion on their being together.

On one especially beautiful August day they paced side by side, talking at moments with something of their old tenderness. The sky above the dark-green barriers on either hand was a bottomless deep of blue. The yew-boughs were covered in curious profusion by the handiwork of energetic spiders, who had woven their glistening webs in every variety of barbaric pattern. In shape some resembled hammocks, others purses, others deep bags, in the middle of which a large yellow insect remained motionless and watchful.

'Shall we sit for a little while in the summer-house?' said Rosalys at last, in flat accents, for a *tête-à-tête* with Jim had long ceased to give her any really strong beats of pleasure. 'I want to talk to you further about plans; how often we had better write, and so on.'

They sat down in an arbour made of rustic logs which overlooked the mere. The woodwork had been left rough within, and dusty spider-webs hung in the crevices; here and there the bark had fallen away in strips; above, on the roof, there were clumps of fungi, looking like tufts of white fur.

'This is a sunless, queer sort of place you have chosen,' he said, looking round critically.

The boughs had grown so thickly in the foreground that the glittering margin of water was hardly perceptible between their interlacing twigs, and no visible hint of a human habitation was given, though the rustic shelter had been originally built with the view of affording a picturesque glimpse of the handsome old brick house, wherein the Ambroses had lived for some three centuries.

'You might have found a more lively scene for what will be, perhaps, our last interview for years,' Jim went on.

'Are you really going so soon?' she asked, passing over the complaint.

'Next week. And my father has made all sorts of arrangements for me. Besides, he is beginning to suspect that you and I are rather too intimate. And your mother knows, somehow or other, that I have been up several times of late. We must be careful.'

'I suppose so,' she answered absently, looking

out under the log-roof at a chaffinch swinging himself backwards and forwards on a large bough. A sort of dreary indifference to her surroundings; a sense of being caged and trapped had begun to take possession of Rosalys. The present was full of perplexity, the future objectless. Now and then, when she looked at Jim's lithe figure, and healthy, virile face, she felt that perhaps she might have been able to love him still if only he had cared for her with a remnant of his former passionate devotion. But his indifference was even more palpable than her own. They sat and talked on within the dim arbour for a little while. Then Jim made one of the unfortunate remarks that always galled her to the quick. She rose in anger, answered him with cold sarcasm, and hastened away down the little wood. He followed her, a rather ominous light shining in his eyes.

'Your temper is really growing insufferable, Rosalys!' he cried, and clenched his hand roughly on her arm to detain her.

'How dare you!' said the girl. 'For God's sake leave me, and don't come back again! I rejoice to think that in a few days it will not be in your power to insult me any more!'

'Damn it—I am going to leave you, am I not? I only want to keep you here for a moment to come to some understanding! Indeed, you'll be surprised to find how very much I am going to leave you, when you hear what I mean! My ideas have grown considerably emancipated of late, and therefore I tell you there is no reason on earth why any soul should ever know of that miserable mistake we made in the spring.'

She winced a little; it was an unexpected move; and her eyes lingered uneasily on a copper-coloured butterfly playing a game of hide-and-seek with a little blue companion.

'Who,' he continued, 'is ever going to search the register of that old East-London church? We must philosophically look on the marriage as an awkward fact in our lives, which won't prevent our loving anybody else when we feel inclined. In my opinion this early error will carry one advantage with it—that we shall be unable to extinguish any love we may feel for another person by a sordid matrimonial knot—unless, indeed, after seven years of obliviousness to one another's existence.'

'I'll—try to—emancipate myself likewise,' she said slowly. 'It will be well to forget this tragedy of our lives! And the most tragic part of it is—that we are not even sorry that we don't love each other any more!'

'The truest words you ever spoke!'

'And the surest event that was ever to come, given your nature.'

'And yours!'

She hastened on down the grass walk into the broad gravelled path leading to the house. At the corner stood Mrs. Ambrose, who was better, and had come out for a stroll—assuming as an invalid the privilege of wearing a singular scarlet gown, and a hat in which a number of black quills stood startlingly erect.

'Ah—Rosy!' she cried. 'Oh, and Mr. Durrant? What a colour you have got, child!'

'Yes. Mr. Durrant and I have been having a furious political discussion, mamma. I have grown quite hot over it. He is more unreasonable than ever. But when he gets abroad he won't be as he is now. A few years of India will change all that.' And to carry on the idea of her unconcern she turned to whistle to a bold robin that had flitted down from a larch-tree, perched on the yew hedge, and looked inquiringly at her, answering her whistle with his pathetic little pipe.

Durrant had come up behind. 'Yes,' he said cynically. 'One never knows how an enervating country may soften one's brains.'

He bade them a cool good-bye and left. She watched his retreating figure, the figure of the active, the strong, the handsome animal, who had scarcely won the better side of her nature at all. He never turned his head. So this was the end!

The bewildering bitterness of it well-nigh

paralysed Rosalys for a few moments. Why had they been allowed—he and she—to love one another with that eager, resistless passion, and then to part with less interest in each other than ordinary friends? She felt ashamed of having ceded herself to him. If her mother had not been beside her she would have screamed out aloud in her exasperating pain.

Mrs. Ambrose lifted up her voice. 'What are you looking at, child? . . . My dear, I want a little word with you. Are you sure you are attending? When you pout your lip like that, Rosalys, I always know that you are in a bad frame of mind. . . . The vicar has been here; and he has made me a little unhappy.'

'I should have thought he was too stupid to give any one a pang! Why do they put such simpletons into the churches?'

'Well—he says that people are chattering about you and that young Durrant. And I must tell you that—that, from a marrying point of view, he is impossible. You know that. And I don't want him to make up to you. Now, Rosalys, my darling, tell me honestly—I feel I have not looked after you lately as I ought to have done—tell me honestly: Is he in love with you?'

'He is not, mother, to my certain knowledge.'

'Are you with him?'

'No. That I swear.'

CHAPTER V

SEVEN years and some months had passed since Rosalys spoke as above-written. And never a sound of Jim.

As she had mentally matured under the touch of the gliding seasons, Miss Ambrose had determined to act upon the hint Jim had thrown out to her as to the practical nullity of their marriage contract if they simply kept in different hemispheres without a word. She had never written to him a line; and he had never written a line to her.

He might be dead for all that she knew; he possibly was dead. She had taken no steps to ascertain anything about him, though she had been aware for years that his name was no longer in the Army List. Dead or alive he was completely cut off from the county in which he and she had lived, for his father had died a long time before this, his house and properties had been sold, and not a scion of the house of Durrant remained in that part of England.

Rosalys had readily imbibed his ideas of their mutual independence; and now, after the lapse of all these years, had acted upon them with the surprising literalness of her sex when they act upon advice at all.

Mrs. Ambrose, who had distinguished herself

in no whit during her fifty years of life saving by the fact of having brought a singularly beautiful girl into the world, had passed quietly out of it. Rosalys's uncle had succeeded his sister-in-law in the possession of the old house with its red tower, and the broad paths and garden-lands; he had been followed by an unsatisfactory son of his, last in the entail, and thus unexpectedly Rosalys Ambrose found herself sole mistress of the spot of her birth.

People marvelled somewhat that she continued to call herself Miss Ambrose. Though a woman now getting on for thirty, sne was remarkably attractive both in face and in figure, and could confront the sunlight as well as the moonbeams still. In the manner of women who are yet sure of their charms she was fond of representing herself as much older than she really was. Perhaps she would have been disappointed if her friends had not laughed and contradicted her, and told her that she was still lovely and looked like a young girl. Lord Parkhurst, anyhow, was firmly of that contradictory opinion; and perhaps she cared more for his views than for any one else's at the present time.

That distinguished sailor had been but one of many suitors; but he had stirred her heart as none of the others could do. It was not merely that he was brave, and pleasing, and had returned from a campaign in Egypt with a hero's reputation; but that his chivalrous feelings towards women, originating perhaps in the fact that he knew very little about them, were sufficient to gratify the most exacting of the sex.

His rigid notions of duty and honour, both towards them and from them, made the blood of Rosalys run cold when she thought of a certain little episode of her past life, notwithstanding that, or perhaps because, she loved him dearly.

'He is not the least bit of a flirt, like most sailors,' said Miss Ambrose to her cousin and companion, Miss Jennings, on a particular afternoon in the eighth year of Jim Durrant's obliteration from her life. It was an afternoon with an immense event immediately ahead of it; no less an event than Rosalys's marriage with Lord Parkhurst, which was to take place on the very next day.

The local newspaper had duly announced the coming wedding in proper terms as 'the approaching nuptials of the beautiful and wealthy Miss Ambrose, of Ambrose Towers, with a distinguished naval officer, Lord Parkhurst.' There followed an ornamental account of the future bridegroom's heroic conduct during the late war. 'The handsome face and figure of Lord Parkhurst,' wound up the honest paragraphist, 'are not altogether unknown to us in this vicinity, as he has recently been visiting his uncle, Colonel Lacy, High Sheriff of the county. We wish all prosperity to the happy couple, who have doubtless a brilliant and cloudless future before them.'

This was the way in which her acceptance of Durrant's views had worked themselves out. He had said: 'After seven years of mutual oblivion we can marry again if we choose.'

And she had chosen.

Rosalys almost wished that Lord Parkhurst had been a flirt, or at least had won experience as the victim of one, or many, of those precious creatures, and had not so implicitly trusted her. It would have brought things more nearly to a level.

'A flirt! I should think not,' said Jane Jennings. 'In fact, Rosalys, he is almost alarmingly strict in his ideas. It is a mistake to believe that so many women are angels, as he does. He is too simple. He is bound to be disappointed some day.'

Miss Ambrose sighed nervously. 'Yes,' she said.

'I don't mean by you to-morrow! God forbid!'

'No.'

Miss Ambrose sighed again, and a silence followed, during which, while recalling unutterable things of the past, Rosalys gazed absently out of the window at the lake, that some men were dredging; the mud, left bare by draining down the water, being imprinted with hundreds of little footmarks of plovers feeding there. Eight or nine herons stood further away, one or two composedly fishing, their grey figures reflected with unblurred clearness in the mirror of the pool. Some little water-hens waddled with a fussy gait across the sodden ground in front of them, and a procession of wild geese came through the sky, and passed on till they faded away into a row of black dots.

Suddenly the plovers rose into the air, uttering their customary wails, and dispersing like a group of stars from a rocket; and the herons drew up their flail-like legs, and flapped themselves away.

Something had disturbed them; a carriage sweeping round to the other side of the house.

'There's the door-bell!' Rosalys exclaimed, with a start. 'That's he, it must be! Is my hair untidy, Jane? I've been rumpling it awfully, leaning back on the cushions. And do see if my gown is all right at the back—it never did fit well.'

The butler flung open the folding doors, and announced in the voice of a man who felt that it was quite time for this nonsense of calling to be put an end to by the more compact arrangement of the morrow—

'Lord Parkhurst!'

A man of middle size, with a fair and pleasant face, and a short beard, entered the room. His blue eyes smiled rather more than his lips as he took the little hand of his hostess in his own with the air of one verging on proprietorship of the same, and said: 'Now, darling; about what we have to settle before the morning! I have come entirely on business, as you perceive.'

Rosalys tenderly smiled up at him. Miss Jennings left the room, and Rosalys's sailor silently kissed and admired his betrothed, till he continued—

'Ah—my beautiful one! I have nothing to give you in return for the immeasurable gift you are about to bestow on me—excepting such love as no man ever felt before! I almost wish you were not quite so good, and perfect, and innocent as you are! And I wish you were a poorer woman—as poor as I—and had no lovely home such as this. To think you have rejected all other men for such an unworthy fellow as me!'

Rosalys looked away from him along the green vistas of chestnuts and beeches stretching far down outside the windows.

'Oswald—I know how much you care for

me; and that is why I—hope you won't be disappointed—after you have taken me to-morrow for good and all! I wonder if I shall hinder and hamper you in your profession? Perhaps you ought to marry a girl much younger than yourself—your nature is so young—not a maturing woman like me.'

For all answer he smiled at her with the confiding, fearless gaze that she loved.

Lord Parkhurst stayed on through a paradisiacal hour till Miss Jennings came to tell them that tea was in the library. Presently they were reminded by the same faithful relative and dependant that on that evening of all evenings they had promised to drive across to the house of Colonel Lacy, Lord Parkhurst's uncle, and one of Rosalys's near neighbours, and dine there quietly with two or three intimate friends.

CHAPTER VI

WHEN Rosalys entered Colonel Lacy's drawing-room before dinner, the eyes of the few guests assembled there were naturally enough fixed upon her.

'By Jove, she's better looking than ever—though she's not more than a year or two under thirty!' whispered young Lacy to a man standing in the shadow behind a high lamp.

The person addressed started, and did not answer for a moment. Then he laughed and said forcedly—

'Yes, wonderfully handsome she certainly is.'

As he spoke his hostess, a fat and genial lady, came blandly towards him.

'Mr. Durrant, I'm so sorry we've no lady for you to take in to-night. One or two people have thrown us over. I want to introduce you to Miss Ambrose. Isn't she lovely? Oh, how stupid I am! Of course you grew up in this neighbourhood, and must have known all about her as a girl.'

Jim Durrant it was, in the flesh; once the soldier, now the 'traveller and explorer' of the little-known interior of Asiatic countries, to use the words in which he described himself. His foreign-looking and sun-dried face was rather pale and set as he walked last into the dining-room with young Lacy. He had only arrived on that day at an hotel in the nearest town, where he had been accidentally met and recognised by that young man, and asked to dinner offhand.

Smiling, and apparently unconscious, he sat down on the left side of his hostess, talking calmly to her and across the table to the one or two whom he knew. Rosalys heard his voice as the phantom of a dead sound mingling with the usual trivial words and light laughter of the rest—Lord Parkhurst's conversation about Egyptian finance, and Mrs. Lacy's platitudes about the Home Rule question—as if she were living through a curiously incoherent dream.

Suddenly during the progress of dinner Mrs. Lacy looked across with a glance of solicitude towards the other end of the table, and said in a low voice—

'I am afraid Miss Ambrose is rather overstrained—as she may naturally be? She looks *so* white and tired. Do you think, Parkhurst, that she finds this room too hot? I will have the window opened at the top.'

'She does look pale,' Lord Parkhurst murmured, and as he spoke glanced anxiously and tenderly towards his betrothed. 'I think, too, she has a little overtaxed herself—she doesn't usually get so white as this.'

Rosalys felt his eyes upon her, looked across at him, and smiled strangely.

When dinner was ended Rosalys still seemed not quite herself, whereupon she was taken in hand by her good and fussy hostess; sal-volatile was brought, and she was given the most comfortable chair and the largest cushions the house afforded. It seemed to Rosalys as if hours had elapsed before the men joined the ladies, and there came that general moving of places like the shuffling of a pack of cards. She heard Jim's voice speaking close to her ear—

'I want to have a word with you.'

'I can't!' she faltered.

'Did you get my letter?'

'No,' said she.

'I wonder how that was! Well—I'll be at the door of Ambrose Towers while the stable-clock is striking twelve to-night. Be there to meet me. I'll not detain you long. We must have an understanding.'

'For God's sake how do you come here?'

'I saw in the newspapers that you were going to marry. What could I do otherwise than let you know I was alive?'

'Oh, you might have done it less cruelly!'

'Will you be at the door?'

'I *must*, I suppose! . . . Don't tell him here —before these people! It will be such an agonising disturbance that——'

Of course I shan't. Be there.'

This was all they could say. Lord Parkhurst came forward, and observing to Durrant 'They are wanting you for bézique,' sat down beside Rosalys.

She had intended to go home early, and went even earlier than she had planned. At half-past ten she found herself in her own hall, not knowing how she had got there, or when she had bidden adieu to Lord Parkhurst, or what she had said to him.

Jim's letter was lying on the table awaiting her.

As soon as she had got upstairs and slipped into her dressing-gown, had despatched her maid, and ascertained that all the household had retired, she read her husband's note, which briefly informed her that he had led an adventurous life since they had parted, and had come back to see if she were living, when he suddenly heard that she was going to be married. Then Rosalys sat down at her writing-table to begin somehow a letter to Lord Parkhurst. To write that was an imperative duty, before she slept. It need not be said that awful indeed to her was its object—the letting Lord Parkhurst know that she had a husband, and had seen him that day. But she could not shape a single line; and the visioned aspect that she would wear in his eyes as soon as he discovered the truth of her history was so terrible to her that she burst into hysterical sobbing over the paper as she sat.

The clock crept on to twelve before Rosalys had written a word. The labour seemed Herculean—insuperable. Why had she not told him face to face?

Twelve o'clock it was, and nothing done; and controlling herself as women can when they must, she went down to the door. Softly opening it a little way she saw against the iron gate immediately without it the form of her husband, Jim Durrant—upon the whole much the same form she had known eight years ago.

'Here I am,' said he.

'Yes,' said she.

'Open this iron thing.'

A momentary feeling of aversion caused her to hesitate.

'Do you hear—do you mean to say—Rosalys!' he began.

'No—no. Of course I will!' She opened the grille and he came up and touched her hand lightly.

'A kiss is not allowed, I suppose,' he observed, with a mock solemnity, 'in view of the fact that you are to be married to-morrow?'

'You know better,' she said, 'Of course I'm not going to commit bigamy! The wedding is not to be.'

'Have you explained it to him?'

'N—no—not yet. I was just writing it when——'

'Ha—you haven't! Good. Woman's way. Shall I give him a friendly call to-morrow morning?'

'Oh, no, no—let me do it!' she implored. I love him so well, and it will break his heart if it is not done gently! O God—if I could only die to-night, while he still believes in me! You don't know what affection I have felt for him!' she continued miserably, not caring what Jim thought. 'He has been my whole world! And he—he believes me to be so good! He has all the old-fashioned ideas of marriage that people of your fast set smile at! He knows nothing of any kind of former acquaintance between you and me. I ought not to have done it—kept him in the dark! I tried not to. But I was so fearfully lonely! And now I've lost him! ... If I could only have got at that register in that City church, how I would have torn out the leaf!' she added vehemently.

'That's a pleasant remark to make to a husband!'

'Well—that was my feeling; I may as well be honest! I didn't know you were coming back any more; and you yourself suggested that I might be able to re-marry!'

'You'd better do it—I shan't tell. And if anybody else did, the punishment is not heavy nowadays. The judges are beginning to discountenance informers on previous marriages, if the new-assorted couples themselves are satisfied to forget them.'

'Don't insult me so. You've not forgotten how to do that in all these years!'

There was a silence, in which she with

passive gloom regarded the familiar scene before her. The inquisitive jays, the pensive wood-doves, that lodged at their ease thereabouts, as if knowing that their proprietor was a gunless woman, all slept calmly, and not a creature was conscious of the presence of these two but a little squirrel they had disturbed in a beech near the shady wall. Durrant remained gazing at her; then he spoke, in a changed and richer voice—

'Rosalys!'

She looked vaguely at his face without answering.

'How pretty you look in this starlight—much as you did when we used to meet here nine or ten years ago!'

'Ah! But——'

'... Let me sit down in your hall, or somewhere, Rosalys! I've come a long way to-day, and I'm tired. And after eight years!'

'I don't know what to say to it—there's no light downstairs! The servants may hear us, too—it is not so very late.'

'We can whisper. And suppose they do? They must know to-morrow.'

She gasped a sigh and preceded him in through the door.

'Yes, they must!' she said.

CHAPTER VII

WHEN they re-appeared the lawn was as silent as when they had left it, though the sleep of things had weakened down to a certain precarious slightness, and round the corner of the house a low line of light showed the dawn.

'Now, good-bye, dear,' said her husband lightly. 'You'll let him know at once?'

'Of course.'

'And send to me directly after?'

'Yes.'

'And now for my walk across the fields to the hotel. These boots are thin, but I know the old way well enough. By Jove, I wonder what Mélanie——'

'Who?'

'Oh—what Mélanie will think, I was going to say. It slipped out. I didn't mean to hurt your feelings at all.'

'Mélanie—who is she?'

'Well—she's a French lady. You know, of course, Rosalys, that I thought you were perhaps dead—and—so this lady passes as Mrs. Durrant.'

Rosalys started.

'In fact I found her in the East, and took pity upon her—that's all. Though if it had happened that you had not been living now I have got back, I should have married her at once, of course.'

'Is—she, then, here with you at the hotel?'

'Oh no—I wouldn't bring her on here till I knew how things were.'

'Then where is she?'

'I left her at my rooms in London. Oh, it will be all right—I shall see her safely back to Paris, and make a little provision for her. Nobody in England knows anything of her existence.'

'When—did you part from her?'

'Well, of course, at breakfast-time.'

Rosalys bowed herself against the doorway, and Jim was almost distressed when he saw the distortion of her agonised face.

'Now why should you take on like this! There's nothing in it. People do these things. Living in a prim society here you don't know how the world goes on!'

'Oh, but to think it didn't occur to me that the sort of man——'

Jim, though anxious, seemed to awaken to something humorous in the situation, and vented a momentary chuckle. 'Well, it is rather funny that I should have let it out. But still——'

'Don't make a deep wrong deeper by cruel levity. Go away!'

'You'll be in a better mood to-morrow,

mark me ; and then I'll tell you all my history. There—I'm gone! *Au revoir!*'

He disappeared under the trees. Rosalys, rousing herself, closed the gate and fastened the door, and sat down in one of the hall chairs, her teeth shut tight, and her little hands clenched. When she had passed this mood, and returned upstairs, she bent again over her writing-table and wept.

But in a few minutes she found herself nerved to an unexpected and passionate vigour of action, and began writing her letter to Lord Parkhurst with great rapidity. Sheet after sheet she filled, and having read them over, she sealed up the letter and placed it on the mantel-piece to be given to a groom and despatched by hand as soon as the morning was a little further advanced.

With cold feet and a burning head she flung herself upon the bed just as she was, and waited for the day without the power to sleep. When she had lain nearly two hours, and the morning had crept in and she could hear from the direction of the stables that the men were astir, she rang for her maid, and, taking the letter in her hand, stood with it in an attitude of suspense as the woman entered. The latter looked full of intelligence.

'Are any of the men about?' asked Rosalys.
'Yes. ma'am. There have been such an

accident in the Meads this past night—about half a mile down the river—and Jones ran up from the lodge to call for help quite early; and Benton and Peters went as soon as they were dressed. A gentleman drowned—yes—it's Mr. James Durrant—the son of Mr. Durrant who died some years ago. He came home only yesterday, after having been heard nothing of for years and years. He left Mrs. Durrant, who they say is a French lady, somewhere in London, but they have telegraphed and found her, and she's coming. They say she's quite distracted. The poor gentleman left the Three Lions last night and went out to dinner, saying he would walk home, as it was a fine night and not very far; and it is supposed he took the old short cut across the moor where there used to be a path when he was a lad at home, crossing the big river by a plank. There is only a rail now, and he must have tried to get across upon it, for it was broken in two, and his body found in the water-weeds just below.'

'Is he—dead?'

'Oh yes. They had a great trouble to get him out. The men have just come from carrying him to the hotel. It will be sad for his poor wife when she gets there.'

'His poor wife—yes.'

'Travelling all the way from London on such an errand!'

Rosalys had allowed the hand in which she held the letter to Lord Parkhurst to drop to her side; she now put it in the pocket of her dressing-gown.

'I was wishing to send somewhere,' she said. 'But I think I shall wait till later.'

The house was astir betimes on account of the wedding, and Rosalys's companion in particular, who was not sad because she was going to live on with the bride. When Miss Jennings saw her cousin's agitation she said she looked ill, and insisted upon sending for the doctor. He, who was the local practitioner, arrived at breakfast-time; very proud to attend such an important lady, who usually got doctored in London. He said that Rosalys was not quite in her ordinary state of health, prescribed a tonic, and declared that she would be all right in an hour or two. He then informed her that he had been suddenly called up that morning about the case of which they had possibly heard—the drowning of Mr. Durrant.

'And you could do nothing?' asked Rosalys.

'Oh no. He'd been under water too long for any human aid. Dead and stiff. . . . It was not so very far down from here. . . . Yes, I remember him quite as a boy. But he has had no relations hereabout for years past—old Durrant's property was sold to pay his debts, if you recollect; and nobody expected to see the son again. I think he has lived in the East Indies a good deal. Much better for him if he had not come—poor fellow.'

When the doctor had left, Rosalys went to the window, and remained for some time thinking. There was the lake from which the water had flowed down to the river that had drowned Jim after visiting her last night—as a mere interlude in his life with the Frenchwoman Mélanie. She turned, took from her dressing-gown pocket the renunciatory letter to her intended husband, Lord Parkhurst, thrust it through the bars of the grate, and watched it till it was entirely consumed.

The wedding had been fixed for an early hour in the afternoon, and as the morning wore on Rosalys felt increasing strength, mental and physical. The doctor's dose had been a powerful one; the image of Mélanie, too, had much to do with her recuperative mood; more still Rosalys's innate qualities, the nerve of the woman who nine years earlier had gone to the city to be married as if it were a mere shopping expedition; most of all, she loved Lord Parkhurst; he was the man among all men she desired. Rosalys allowed things to take their course.

Soon the dressing began; and she sat through it quite calmly. When Lord Parkhurst rode across for a short visit that day he only noticed that she seemed strung-up, nervous, and that the flush of love which mantled her cheek died away to pale rather quickly.

On the way to church the road skirted the low-lying ground where the river was, and about a dozen men were seen in the bright-green meadow, standing beside the deep central stream, and looking intently at a broken rail.

'Who are those men?' said the bride.

'Oh—they are the coroner's jury, I think,' said Miss Jennings, 'come to view the place where the unfortunate Mr. Durrant lost his life last night. It was curious that, by the merest accident, he should have been at Mrs. Lacy's dinner—since they hardly knew him at all.'

'It was—I saw him there,' said Rosalys.

Ten minutes later she was kneeling against the altar railings, with Lord Parkhurst on her right hand.

The wedding was by no means a gay one, and there were few people invited, Rosalys, for one thing, having hardly any relations. The newly united pair got away from the house very soon after the ceremony. When they drove off there was a group of people round the door, and some among the bystanders asked how far they were going that day.

'To Dover. They cross the Channel to-morrow, I believe.'

To-morrow came, and those who had gathered

together at the wedding went about their usual duties and amusements, Colonel Lacy among the rest. As he and his wife were returning home by the late afternoon train after a short journey up the line, he bought a copy of an evening paper, and glanced at the latest telegrams.

'My good God!' he cried.

'What?' said she, starting towards him.

He tried to read—then handed the paper; and she read for herself—

'DOVER.—DEATH OF LORD PARKHURST, R.N.

'We regret to announce that this distinguished nobleman and heroic naval officer, who arrived with Lady Parkhurst last evening at the Lord Chamberlain Hotel in this town, preparatory to starting on their wedding-tour, entered his dressing-room very early this morning, and shot himself through the head with a revolver. The report was heard shortly after dawn, none of the inmates of the hotel being astir at the time. No reason can be assigned for the rash act.'

THE END.